BEST-LOVED
HUMOR OF THE LDS
PEOPLE

BEST-LOVED HUMOR OF THE LDS PEOPLE

* * *

Edited by Linda Ririe Gundry, Jay A. Parry,
and Jack M. Lyon

DESERET BOOK COMPANY

SALT LAKE CITY, UTAH

Appreciation is expressed to Edward L. Kimball for graciously granting permission to use many anecdotes from the life of his father, President Spencer W. Kimball. We acknowledge copyright holders whose material we may have included but with whom we were unable to make personal contact. Other works are in public domain. If any acknowledgments have been overlooked, please notify the publisher and omissions will be rectified in future editions.

Library of Congress Cataloging-in-Publication Data

Best-loved humor of the LDS people / edited by Linda Ririe Gundry, Jay A. Parry, and Jack M. Lyon.
    p.   cm.
Includes bibliographical references and index.
ISBN 1-57345-396-X
    1. Church of Jesus Christ of Latter-day Saints—Humor. 2. Mormon Church—Humor. I. Gundry, Linda Ririe. II. Parry, Jay A. III. Lyon, Jack M.
BX8638.B47   1999
289.3'32'0207—dc21   98-56101
                                               CIP

Printed in the United States of America   72082-6380
10 9 8 7 6 5 4 3

"Now unless you should think that I am going to be really serious, I would like to have you smile because after all we must keep a sense of humor whatever comes. I think of all the people in the world [Latter-day Saints] should be the happiest. We have the greatest and most joyous message in the world."

—HUGH B. BROWN

CONTENTS

* * *

Contents

CONTENTS

CONTENTS

Contents

PREFACE

* * *

"One must have a sense of humor to be an optimist in times like these," Hugh B. Brown once said. "And you young women will need a sense of humor if you marry these young men and try to live with them. Golden Kimball once said in a conference, 'The Lord Himself must like a joke or he wouldn't have made some of you people.' But your good humor must be real, not simulated. Let your smiles come from the heart and they will become contagious. You may see men on the street any day whose laugh is only a frozen grin with nothing in it but teeth. Men without humor tend to forget their source, lose sight of their goal, and with no lubrication in their mental crankshafts, they must drop out of the race. Lincoln said, 'Good humor is the oxygen of the soul.' And someone paraphrased, 'The surly bird catches the germ'" (*The Abundant Life* [Salt Lake City: Bookcraft, 1965], 50).

Everybody loves a good joke. Whether we're giving a talk in sacrament meeting, teaching a Sunday School lesson, or presenting a family home evening message, we instinctively turn to humor to bridge the gap between speaker and listeners. Humor lets us see life's bright side, gives us new perspective, and allows us to laugh at our own foibles.

Best-Loved Humor of the LDS People is an extensive collection of oft-repeated jokes, true anecdotes, and quotations that have become or may become favorites among members of the Church. Because humor is so subjective, we have selected a broad variety of material—from mildly to wildly humorous, from one-liners to stories. Included are true incidents from Church history, gently humorous quotations from general conference addresses, and a broad variety of jokes.

Thomas Carlyle stated: "True humor springs not more from the head than from the heart. It is not contempt. Its essence is love. Its issue is not in laughter, but in still smiles which lie far deeper" (Quoted in *BYU Speeches of the Year,* 17 Mar. 1981, 47). Some humor does indeed result in quiet smiles, while some makes us laugh out loud. What's more, when it comes to jokes, one person's "chuckler" is another person's "groaner." We have considered each item in this collection in terms of its possible appeal to different readers, its usefulness and appropriateness for LDS speakers and teachers, and its overall fun value.

As in *Best-Loved Poems of the LDS People* and *Best-Loved Stories of the LDS People,* material in this volume is arranged by topic for easy reference. Within each topic, entries are clearly identified as jokes, quotations, poems, or stories.

We gratefully acknowledge our debt to other compilers and editors. Because jokes are frequently retold, altered, and adapted, it would be impossible for us to identify the original authors or sources of jokes. In the case of quotations and anecdotes, however, we have made every effort to credit the original source where possible. We express our heartfelt appreciation to Ronald A. Millett, Sheri Dew, Kent Ware, Jennifer Adams, Patricia J. Parkinson, and Ronald O. Stucki at Deseret Book Company.

ACCOUNTABILITY

If we could kick the person who is responsible for most of our troubles, we wouldn't be able to sit down for six months.

* * *

A chaplain was walking through a prison and noticed a number of prisoners sewing laundry bags. He walked up to one prisoner and asked, "Sewing, are you?"

"No," said the prisoner sadly. "I'm reaping."

* * *

Police officer at scene of accident: Whose fault was this collision?

Bystander: Neither driver was at fault, sir. They hit each other at exactly the same time.

* * *

The judge looked at the defendant. "Young man, it is alcohol that is responsible for your present sorry state."

"I'm glad you said that. Everyone else says it's my fault."

* * *

As one person explained it, no one wanted to take responsibility for what happened in the Garden of Eden: "Adam blamed Eve, and Eve blamed the snake, and the snake didn't have a leg to stand on."

* * *

The bishop of a struggling little ward worried that the members were not living the gospel. So every week at the end of sacrament meeting he took a few minutes to exhort the people to greater

1

diligence. One old man in the congregation was especially incorrigible. He was known to have a drink now and then, the bishop could smell cigarette smoke on his breath, and the fellow's language was always foul. One day the bishop spoke briefly about staying away from alcoholic beverages. After the meeting, the old man came up to him and said, "Boy, Bishop! You sure told *them!*"

Discouraged that the old man hadn't gotten the point, the bishop was even plainer the next Sunday as he spoke about drinking and smoking. Again the old man missed the point: "Wow, Bishop! You *really* told them today!"

The next Sunday there was a tremendous snowstorm, and no one showed up for church except the bishop and this one incorrigible old man. So the bishop took the whole sacrament meeting, and he spoke about drinking, smoking, and foul language. The old man could have no doubt that he was the target of the bishop's blunt remarks.

After the service, the old man came up to the bishop and said, "Boy oh boy, Bishop! You really told 'em today—if only they'd a been here!"

* Q U O T A T I O N S *

J. Golden Kimball: I know a good deal more about this Church than the man did, one of those strangers that come in our midst, who went on a hill here recently and stood in an ant bed, and when the ants commenced to bite he commenced to curse the "Mormons." I suppose he thought they were "Mormon" ants, and he held us responsible for them (Conference Report, Oct. 1904, 57).

ACTION

* QUOTATIONS *

George A. Smith: There was [a man] by the name of Hawley. He was attacked by a spirit of revelation, somewhere in the State of New York, while he was ploughing; and it took him in such a hurry that he had not time to put on his boots, but travelled barefoot to Kirtland, some six hundred miles distant, to warn Joseph that he was a fallen Prophet; that God had cut Joseph off, and placed in his stead a man by the name of Noah; and the reason Joseph was cut off was, he had suffered the men to wear cushions on their coat sleeves, and the women to wear caps. He went through the streets of Kirtland with a dismal howl, crying, "Woe, woe to the people." On one occasion, about midnight, Brigham Young went out, and took with him a cowhide, and said to Hawley, "If you don't quit annoying the people with your noise, I will cowhide you;" upon which he concluded he had suffered persecution enough for his master's sake, and shut up his noise (*Journal of Discourses* 7:114).

* * *

J. Golden Kimball: It is not very difficult for a Latter-day Saint to believe all that has been revealed. To me it is all true, but the great trouble I am having is to make it work (Conference Report, Apr. 1915, 133).

* STORIES *

King James the First would say to the lords of his council, after they sat upon any great matter, "Well, you have sat, but what have you hatched?"

* * *

A little girl anxiously told her mother that her brother was setting traps for birds. "He won't catch any birds in his traps, will he, Mother?" she asked.

The mother said, "Perhaps he will—you cannot be sure he will not."

"I have prayed about it and asked Heavenly Father to protect the birds," the girl said. Then, becoming more positive, she said, "I *know* he won't catch any."

The mother asked, "How can you be so positive?"

"Because after I said my prayers, I went out and kicked those old traps to pieces" (Packer, *Teach Ye Diligently*, 255).

ADVERSITY

* JOKES *

A worker was leaning far out over the edge of a high building in the middle of a crowded city. *Unfortunately,* he slipped and fell. *Fortunately,* there was a haywagon proceeding slowly down the avenue just below him. *Unfortunately,* there was a pitchfork sticking, prongs up, in the middle of the load of hay. *Fortunately,* the man didn't hit the pitchfork. *Unfortunately,* he didn't hit the haywagon either.

* QUOTATIONS *

John Taylor: We feel that we are kind of half comfortable in these valleys of the mountains, but the devil is not dead yet (*Journal of Discourses* 25:347).

* * *

Ebenezer Robinson: We were taken [to prison] on the 28th of November. Winter set in early that season. A considerable snow had fallen, and the weather became severely cold by the first of December. An amusing scene occurred one cold night. Brother Luman Gibbs, of whom we have heretofore spoken, lodged in the same bed with the writer, and after retiring for the night, he put his feet out of the bed and said: "Stay there and freeze, it serves you right; bring me here all the way from Vermont to be in prison for murder and never thought of killing anybody in all my life." The act was so unexpected and so ludicrous, it convulsed his fellow prisoners with laughter, except Parley P. Pratt; he seemed to get out of humor, and gave him a good scolding (*The Return* 2:236).

* * *

David O. McKay: A dog's got to have a few fleas or he wouldn't know he was a dog (Conference Report, Apr. 1962, 83–84).

* * *

J. Golden Kimball: "I will fear no evil, for thou art with me," "there shall no evil happen to the just." You have read those things a thousand times, and so have I; and then we never think of them. . . . When I was sick, I read [a positive thinking book] from lid to lid, and I went trotting around, saying: "Every day, in every way, I am getting better and better." Every morning when I got up I was worse and worse (Conference Report, Apr. 1926, 61).

* STORIES *

After a huge hurricane devastated the West Indies, a bricklayer who was sent to help repair the damage wrote the following letter to his employer:

"Respected Sirs:

"When I got to the building I found that the hurricane had knocked some bricks off the top. So I rigged up a beam with a pulley at the top of the building and hoisted up a couple of barrels full of bricks. When I had fixed the building, there was a lot of bricks left over. I hoisted the barrel back up again and secured the line at the bottom, and then went up and filled the barrel with the extra bricks. Then I went to the bottom and cast off the line. Unfortunately the barrel of bricks was heavier than I was, and before I knew what was happening the barrel started down, jerking me off the ground. I decided to hang on, and halfway up I met the barrel coming down and received a severe blow on the shoulder. I then continued to the top, banging my head against the beam and getting my finger jammed in the pulley. When the barrel hit the ground it bursted its bottom, allowing all the bricks to spill out. I was now heavier than the barrel and so started down again at high speed. Halfway down, I met the barrel coming up and received severe injuries to my shins. When I hit the ground I landed on the bricks, getting several painful cuts from the sharp edges. At this point I must have lost my presence of mind because I let go of the line. The barrel then came down, giving me another heavy blow on the head and putting me in hospital. I respectfully request sick leave" (in *Speeches of the Year,* 25 Sept. 1973, 105–6).

* * *

After recovering from surgery on his vocal cords, Spencer W. Kimball attended a conference in his home territory of Arizona, where he explained his long absence: "I went away to the East and while I was there I fell among thieves and cutthroats. They cut my throat and stole my voice" (Kimball, "Spencer W. Kimball," *BYU Studies* 25[4]: 66).

ADVICE

* JOKES *

Good advice is always the most successful when it follows a bad scare.

* STORIES *

During the great depression, a prominent banker approached J. Golden Kimball, who was known to swear on occasion. "Brother Kimball," he said, "you really shouldn't swear in our Church gatherings."

Elder Kimball had a ready response: "I don't think this is a time for bankers to be giving advice to anybody" (Cheney, *Golden Legacy*, 41).

AGENCY

* JOKES *

A traveling businessman was going through one of the tiniest towns he'd ever seen. He finished his day's business and then ate dinner at the town's only café. As he finished his main course, the waitress asked him if he would like dessert.

"What are the choices?" the diner asked.

"Yes or no," she replied.

* QUOTATIONS *

Abraham Lincoln: When you have got an elephant by the hind legs and he is trying to run away, it's best to let him run.

* * *

Brigham Young: There are those who, when they know that they have liberty to act in a certain manner, do not care about moving in that direction; but if you say that they cannot or shall not, they are then very anxious to do so. That class reminds me of the [man] who loaned his money, and upon learning that the borrower was likely to fail, asked him when he could pay him. The answer was, "To-day, if you wish it." "Why, have you got it?" "Yes." "Oh, if you have got it, I do not want it; but if you have not got it, I want it very bad" (*Journal of Discourses* 7:67).

* STORIES *

A distraught woman came to Brigham Young for advice. "My husband keeps telling me to go to hell," she said. "What should I do about it?"

In his characteristically practical way, he replied, "Don't go" (see West, *Profiles of the Presidents,* 73).

AGING

* JOKES *

Seminary teacher: Bill, when I was your age, I could name all the Church presidents in order.
Bill: Well, sure. Back then there were only two or three.

* * *

Three older sisters were sitting around a table at Relief Society homemaking meeting, working on crafts and chatting.

The first sister said, "You know, I'm getting really forgetful. This morning, I was standing at the top of the stairs, and I couldn't remember whether I had just come up or was about to go down."

The second sister said, "You think that's bad? The other day, I was sitting on the edge of my bed, and I couldn't remember whether I was going to bed or had just woken up!"

The third sister smiled smugly. "Well, my memory's just as good as it's always been—knock on wood." She rapped on the table, then looked up with a startled expression. "Oh," she said, "someone's at the door."

* * *

"I'll be a hundred years old this month," the oldest ward member announced to the bishop. "And I don't have one single enemy in the whole world."

"That's a wonderful attitude," said the bishop.

"Well, Bishop," said the old man, "The truth is, I've outlived every one of 'em."

* * *

You know you're getting old when . . .

After you get it all together, you realize you'd do better if you took it apart.

You get a little winded when you brush your teeth.

You reach the age when you know all the answers but nobody asks any of the questions.

Your crow's feet need orthopedic shoes.

Your appendix scar hits your knee.

While sitting in a rocking chair you have difficulty in getting it started.

After you get out of the shower, you're glad the mirror's fogged up.

You get up in the morning and you have one shoe on and one shoe off and you can't tell whether you are getting up or going to bed (Conference Report, Oct. 1983, 34–35).

* * *

You're never too old to grow up.

* * *

Grandchildren are God's way of rewarding us for growing old.

* * *

A mother and father watched their daughter, all dressed up and wearing a fragrant corsage, as she left for the junior prom with her date. The mother closed the front door and sighed wistfully. "It almost makes me wish we were young and foolish again, dear," she said.

"Hey!" the husband responded brightly. "One out of two ain't bad!"

* Q U O T A T I O N S *

President J. Reuben Clark, age eighty-three, said to the students at BYU, "Recently some students who were questioned reported they felt anyone past teenage was ancient. That set me to thinking and I suppose that, the post-teenagers being ancients, I am not only ante-diluvian . . . , but I am likewise prehistoric. . . . I shrink from the final step—that I am a fossil" (*Speeches of the Year,* 20 Apr. 1954).

* * *

Arwell L. Pierce: I recall with much interest the visit of President George Albert Smith to the Mexican Mission in May of 1946. . . . I was so happy that President Smith could make that trip, for he seemed to enjoy it immensely. As you may know, President Smith had a keen sense of humor. Well, he was determined to climb to the top of the Pyramid of the Sun, so two missionary Elders, one on either side of the President, helped him climb those many steep steps to the top. About half way up President Smith stopped and with a smile looked at first one then the other Elder and said, "Well, I might help one of you up here, but why should I help two of you?" (Conference Report, Apr. 1951, 112–13).

* * *

German E. Ellsworth: Three years ago in President [J. Reuben] Clark's office, he said to me, "President Ellsworth, when a car has gone 77,000 miles, the bottom may drop out anytime. You slow down."

Facetiously, I said, "President Clark, I'm not as old as you are."
Then he said, "Well, what is the difference?"
I said, "Six weeks" (Conference Report, Oct. 1951, 95).

* * *

11

J. Golden Kimball: I am very glad that I am not so old as I feel (Conference Report, Apr. 1938, 29).

* S T O R I E S *

A young boy raced up the stairs in the Hotel Utah to catch President David O. McKay just as he was getting off the elevator. He asked President McKay how it felt to be ninety-four years old. The president replied, "It feels great when you consider the alternative" (see *Speeches of the Year,* 5 Feb. 1970).

* * *

After many years away, Spencer W. Kimball visited his home town in Arizona. "Is that direction south?" he asked. Someone told him it was. "I knew it used to be south," he said, "but so many other things have changed since we lived here that I thought they might have changed that, too" (Kimball, "Spencer W. Kimball," *BYU Studies* 25[4]: 69).

* * *

Driving down the road one day, Spencer and Camilla Kimball noticed vultures circling in the sky. "I wonder what they're looking for?" Sister Kimball said. Brother Kimball, who had been through a period of ill health, replied, "They're looking for me!" (Kimball, "Spencer W. Kimball," *BYU Studies* 25[4]: 69).

* * *

Spencer W. Kimball once attended an area conference where the local leader offered thanks that the president was well enough to attend, praying that he would "die in the saddle." The next day at the Church ranch, someone suggested that the Kimballs go horseback riding. President Kimball replied, "I don't know whether I want to or not" (Kimball, "Spencer W. Kimball," *BYU Studies* 25[4]: 69).

* * *

On one occasion, the aging President David O. McKay was driving along when a highway patrolman stopped him for speeding. "Oh, I'm sorry, President McKay," the patrolman said. "I didn't know it was you."

"No, I'm glad for it," President McKay responded. "Some people think I'm slowing down in my old age" (see West, *Profiles of the Presidents,* 229).

* * *

Elder Hugh B. Brown told about having his grandson on his knee. The boy felt the wrinkles on his grandfather's face, looked at his white hair, and asked, "Grandpa Brown, were you on Noah's ark?"

President Brown replied, "No, son, Grand-daddy Brown wasn't on Noah's ark."

"Well," the boy asked, "how come you weren't drowned?" (*Speeches of the Year,* 3 Nov. 1970, 2).

* * *

One of Joseph Fielding Smith's sisters came to visit him on a holiday only to find the elderly man working in his office. She scolded him for not taking a day off, saying, "I want you to go home and take a nap. George Albert Smith, Stephen L Richards, and J. Reuben Clark always did."

"Yes," President Smith countered, "and look where they are now" (Joseph Fielding McConkie, *True and Faithful,* 74).

* * *

A little old lady once approached the elderly Hugh B. Brown. "Oh, President Brown," she said, "I've always wanted you to speak at my funeral."

Smiling, he said, "Sister, if you want me to speak at your funeral, you'd better hurry" (see *Speeches of the Year,* 3 Mar. 1974).

* * *

President Marion G. Romney's good-humored love for his wife Ida was manifested in many ways. He delighted in telling of her hearing loss. Once he tried to get Ida to go to her doctor for a hearing check-up, but she didn't think she needed one. Convinced that there was a problem, but not being able to convince Ida, he finally decided to go see her doctor himself and consult about what should be done.

President Romney explained, "He asked me how bad it was, and I said I didn't know. He told me to go home and find out. The doctor instructed me to go into a far room and speak to her. Then I should move nearer and nearer until she did hear." In this way he could learn how bad the hearing loss was. President Romney went home to try his experiment.

"Following the doctor's instructions, I spoke to her from the bedroom while she was in the kitchen—no answer. I moved nearer and spoke again—no answer. So I went right up to the door of the kitchen and said, 'Ida, can you hear me?'

"She responded, 'What is it, Marion? I've answered you three times'" (adapted from Howard, *Marion G. Romney*, 144–45).

* * *

Hugh B. Brown: During the recent conference held in the Tabernacle in Salt Lake City, after two of the younger brethren of the General Authorities had spoken, I whispered to the President [David O. McKay] and said, "President McKay, I believe this Church is going to carry on after you and I are gone."

He said, "Gone where? I am not going any place." Then he added, "Where are you going?" (*Speeches of the Year*, 10 Oct. 1962, 12–13).

* * *

Oscar W. McConkie, Jr.: With a whisper of his ever-present dry humor President [J. Reuben] Clark complained to me: "Oscar, I can't work as hard as I did when I was seventy-five." He was then only eighty-five years old (*BYU Studies* 13[3]: 452).

* * *

Once a friend saw the aged John Quincy Adams on the street. "And how is John Quincy Adams today?" the friend asked.

"Thank you," the ex-President responded, "John Quincy Adams is well, quite well, I thank you. But the house in which he lives at present is becoming quite dilapidated. It is tottering upon its foundations. Time and the seasons have nearly destroyed it, its roof is pretty well worn out. Its walls are much shattered, and it trembles with every wind. The old tenement is becoming almost uninhabitable, and I think John Quincy Adams will have to move out of it soon. But he himself is quite well."

* * *

Once an elderly neighbor came to J. Golden Kimball for advice. "Brother Kimball," he said, "me and Sister Swensen, we want to get married. What do you think?"

"Well, now, Brother Sorensen, I don't know! Why do you want to get married?"

"Well, you see, we want an heir! I want an heir, and Sister Swensen, she wants an heir too."

Brother Kimball looked the old man up and down. "But Brother Sorensen, how old are you and how old is Sister Swensen?"

"Well now, let me see! I turned seventy-three last May, and Sister Swensen, she will be sixty-two right away now."

"Well, Brother," Elder Kimball replied, "you and Sister Swensen may be heir-minded, but I'm afraid you aren't heir-conditioned" (adapted from Fife and Fife, *Saints of Sage and Saddle*, 307).

ATTENTION

* JOKES *

"Who's absentminded now?" the professor challenged his wife as they were walking home from church. "You left your umbrella in the rack, but I remembered both yours and mine."

And he proudly exhibited both umbrellas.

"But, dear," protested his wife, "neither of us brought an umbrella today."

* QUOTATIONS *

J. Golden Kimball: Think of God. How many of us think of God thirty minutes out of twenty-four hours? There is not one out of five hundred that actually thinks of God and his Son Jesus Christ thirty minutes a day. I do; but the first thing I know, my mind wanders off on something else (Conference Report, Apr. 1926, 62).

* * *

Brigham Young: Study to preserve your bodies in life and health, and you will be able to control your minds. And when you come to meeting, bring your minds with you (*Journal of Discourses* 8:135).

ATTITUDE

* JOKES *

Just before the young army recruit made his first parachute jump, he received instructions from his sergeant: "Now, remember these three things: First of all, count to ten, then pull the first rip cord. And second—if nothing happens, pull the second cord, which releases the auxiliary chute. Third—when you land, our truck will pick up you and your gear."

"Yes, sir," said the recruit and then jumped out of the plane. After counting to ten, he pulled the first cord. The chute didn't open. He pulled the second rip cord, and the chute still didn't open.

"Oh, great," he muttered as he plummeted toward the earth. "Now I suppose that truck won't be there either!"

* * *

Complaining ward member: How can I be thankful, Bishop? What have I got to be thankful for?

Bishop: Surely there must be something.

Complainer: Why, I can't even pay my bills!

Bishop: Then be grateful you're not one of your creditors.

* * *

Optimists stay up to see the new year in. Pessimists stay up to make sure the old year leaves.

* * *

Wife (reading newspaper article): This article says we exercise more than a hundred muscles when we laugh!

Husband: Those doggone fitness experts! They take the fun out of everything, don't they?

17

* Q U O T A T I O N S *

Howard W. Hunter was confined to a wheelchair during his old age. At the beginning of one conference address he remarked, "I notice that the rest of you seem to enjoy the conference sitting down, so I will follow your example" (Conference Report, Oct. 1987, 68).

* * *

"We should not yield or surrender to [physical limitations], or give up in despair with the first twinge of stiffening joints in mind or body," said the apostle Hugh B. Brown. "Life will continue to have an alluring and increasing wealth of interest all the way down its western slopes for him who keeps a cutting edge on his awareness." The apostle suffered a painful medical condition for nearly fifty years, but he somehow managed to preserve his sense of humor, often quoting this poem:

> My bifocals are wonderful
> My hearing aid's a find
> My dentures come in handy
> But how I miss my mind!

(see Van Wagoner and Walker, *A Book of Mormons*, 38–39).

* * *

Orson F. Whitney: The spirit of the gospel is optimistic; it trusts in God and looks on the bright side of things. The opposite or pessimistic spirit drags men down and away from God, looks on the dark side, murmurs, complains, and is slow to yield obedience. There is a story told of two buckets that hung in a well, on either end of a long chain, so that when one went up the other went down, and vice versa. They were both drawing water out of the well, both doing precisely the same kind of work, but one of the buckets was an optimist, and the other was a pessimist. The pessimistic bucket complained of its lot, saying: "It doesn't matter how full I come up, I always go back empty." The optimistic bucket, with a bright smile, retorted: "It doesn't matter how empty I go down, I always come back full." . . . Much depends, you see, upon the spirit in which a thing is viewed (Conference Report, Apr. 1917, 43).

* * *

Moses W. Taylor: I am going to tell you the part of President Smith's talk yesterday that made a great impression on me. It was that we should talk about the good things, and not all the time be talking about evil things. You know some people think it is a virtue to be sick. I met President Duckworth yesterday with a big rag around his neck and told him to take it off, it was a sign he was weak, and we want people to look beautiful and strong. . . . I often think of my father [President John Taylor]. You know he filled many missions in the world, and met many great men and many rich men, among others he met Baron Rothschild. One time Rothschild was traveling around the world and he came to Salt Lake City. Father was just about as poor at that time as he ever was in his life, but he had an old carriage and he got the boys out and we had to polish it and fix it up just as good as we could. He bought thirty cents worth of oil to black the harness, and we blacked the harness and worked at the old carriage and harness for about a day. Finally Baron Rothschild called on him. Father had a big black cloak and a silk hat that he had got in France. He had them cleaned and fixed up, and when he and the Baron walked out of the house to the carriage father looked better to me than Baron Rothschild (Conference Report, Apr. 1913, 36).

* * *

Hugh B. Brown: I would like to have you smile because after all we must keep a sense of humor whatever comes. I think of all the people in the world we should be the happiest. We have the greatest and most joyous message in the world. I think when we get on the other side, someone will meet us with a smile (unless we go to the wrong place and then someone will grin) (*Abundant Life,* 83–84).

* * *

Hugh B. Brown: Let your smiles come from the heart and they will become contagious. You may see men on the street any day whose laugh is only a frozen grin with nothing in it but teeth. Men without humor tend to forget their source, lose sight of their goal, and with no lubrication in their mental crankshafts, they must drop out of the race. Lincoln said, "Good humor is the oxygen of the soul." And someone paraphrased, "The surly bird catches the germ" (*Speeches of the Year,* 24 May 1962, 8).

* * *

J. Golden Kimball: I am trying to be optimistic, and I am having quite a time of it. I cannot work myself up quite as well as the man who fell from a twenty-story building, and as he passed a window of the tenth story, a drummer in the room said to his wife: "Gee, that fellow is optimistic." His wife said, "What do you mean?" "Why, as the fellow passed the window, he said: 'I'm all right yet'" (Conference Report, Apr. 1915, 78).

* * *

Franklin D. Richards: On the green Isle of Ireland, where the poor and afflicted are numerous there are people who have to pay a rent of five pounds an acre for land, and they must raise sufficient off it to support their families, and raise the money to pay the rent. But here we can buy or take up land, and have it, too, for the taking, but some of us consider it an awful job to fence it (*Journal of Discourses* 26:255).

* * *

Brigham Young: The persons who enjoy [the spirit of the gospel] are never sorrowful nor cast down. They never endure afflictions and mourn because they suppose that they have sacrificed for the Gospel, but they are always joyful, always cheerful, with a happy smile on their faces, and, as brother Robert said, it does make the devil mad (*Journal of Discourses* 4:299).

* * *

J. Golden Kimball: I feel happy, just as happy as a man can feel with the rheumatism (Conference Report, Oct. 1906, 117).

* * *

Orson F. Whitney: The fall and winter conferences of the British Mission—fourteen in number, held one week apart—were just beginning, the first one in Ireland, where things were in a turmoil, men being shot down every few minutes or so. I was kind-o'-glad I couldn't go, and Brother Morton was none too happy at being sent. But he went, and had a good time—there's always a good time where Brother Morton goes—and came back rejoicing; the return trip being particularly delightful (Conference Report, Apr. 1924, 37).

* * *

Matthew Cowley: When I was first called to the Council of the Twelve, before one of my visits to the Pacific, President [J. Reuben] Clark called me into his office. I shook hands with him to say goodbye, and he said, "Now, my boy, kid"—he calls me kid—"Now, kid, don't forget rule six." I said, "What's rule six?" He said, "Don't take yourself too darn seriously." I said, "What are the other five?" He said, "There aren't any" (*Matthew Cowley Speaks*, 132–33).

* STORIES *

Elder LeGrand Richards of the Quorum of the Twelve had a droll sense of humor that stayed with him throughout his long life. At a birthday party held in his honor on the occasion of his ninetieth birthday, President N. Eldon Tanner asked Elder Richards, "Have you lived all your life in the United States?"

"Not yet!" answered Elder Richards (Tate, *LeGrand Richards,* 279–80).

* * *

Even in his old age, President David O. McKay retained his sense of courtesy—and his humor. Throughout his life he always rose when Emma, his wife, came into the room.

Robert Lawrence McKay, one of President McKay's sons, recalls that later in life, when both President and Sister McKay were confined to wheelchairs, they would good-humoredly challenge each other to a "race to the elevator" (see West, *Profiles of the Presidents,* 219).

* * *

In her nineties, Camilla Eyring Kimball, wife of President Spencer W. Kimball, noted, "A few months ago I took up painting. When someone asked why, I had to say, 'What else can you take up at ninety-two?'" (Edward L. Kimball, ed., *Writings of Camilla Eyring Kimball,* 137).

* * *

Charles Ora Card founded the Mormon settlement of Cardston, Alberta, on the windswept plains of Canada. One blustery morning, Brother Card was walking to church with his father. "Isn't the air fresh and invigorating?" he asked.

"Yes," said his father, "and isn't there a lot of it?" (see Ward, *New Era,* July 1994, 38).

* * *

As William Dean Howells and Mark Twain were coming out of church one morning, it commenced to rain heavily.

"Do you think it will stop?" asked Howells.

"It always has," answered Twain.

BALDNESS

* QUOTATIONS *

Heber C. Kimball: I have often told you that all my lazy hairs were gone; and I have often told the young Elders, to encourage them, that the first mission I took, after I was ordained one of the Twelve, was through New England and into Nova Scotia, 1500 miles travel on foot with my valise on my back. Soon after I started I found that I was rather unlearned, though I knew that before, but I knew it better after I started.

I began to study the Scriptures, as brother McArthur did, and I had so little knowledge that the exercise of study began to swell my head and open my pores insomuch that the hairs dropped out; and if you will let your minds expand as mine did you will have no hair on your heads. I expected to lose all my hair, and my head too; but I am alive and in the house of Israel; and I expect to live to see this people prosper, the house of Israel gathered, and scattered Israel connected with this people; and we will bring about the purposes of God (*Journal of Discourses* 4:107).

* STORIES *

In 1946 Spencer W. Kimball was chairman of a quarterly social for General Authorities and their wives. For entertainment, he organized a quartet consisting of himself and Ezra Taft Benson, Mark E. Petersen, and Matthew Cowley, with Harold B. Lee at the piano. Elder Kimball had the group learn a comic song about Herpicide, a sure cure for baldness. On the night of their performance, they pulled from the audience LeGrand Richards and Milton R. Hunter, both of whom were bald. Then, as they sang, they rubbed tonic on the men's heads and covered their handiwork with towels wrapped like turbans. At the end of the song, they unwrapped the towels, revealing a red fright wig on one man and barrister's curls on the other (Kimball, "Spencer W. Kimball," *BYU Studies* 25[4]: 61).

BIBLE

* J O K E S *

After the flood, Noah went back to the ark to make sure all of the animals had left. All the stalls were empty, but he found two snakes coiled snuggly in a corner.

"What are you doing here?" he asked. "You're supposed to go forth and multiply."

"We can't," one of them said. "We're adders."

* * *

"Just the same," insisted Noah's wife, "I'd feel a lot better about it if we locked up those termites in a metal box."

* * *

Primary teacher: And then Lot's wife turned back to look, and she suddenly turned into a pillar of salt.

Young class member: That's nothing! One day my dad turned back to look while he was driving, and he turned into a telephone pole!

* * *

A Primary class was studying the Old Testament. When little Jill came home, she said, "Daddy, there's something I don't understand about the Bible. Could I ask you a question?"

"Of course, sweetheart," said her father. "What is it?"

"Well, the children of Israel built the temple, the children of

Israel were slaves of Pharaoh, the children of Israel crossed the Red Sea, the children of Israel got the Ten Commandments from Moses. I just wondered—didn't the grownups do anything?"

* * *

Q: What time of day was Adam created?
A: A little before Eve.

Q: What did Adam and Eve do after they were cast out of the Garden?
A: They raised Cain.

Q: Who was the best financier in the Bible?
A: Noah. He floated his stock while the rest of the world was in liquidation.

Q: What did Noah say to his sons when they were fishing off the side of the ark?
A: You're not using worms, are you?

Q: Where is baseball mentioned in the Bible?
A: When Rebekah carries the pitcher to the well and when the Prodigal Son runs for home.

Q: Where is the first mention of tennis in the Bible?
A: When Joseph served in Pharaoh's court.

Q: What made Pharaoh's daughter such a financier?
A: She pulled a prophet from the rush on the bank.

Q: Besides Adam, who does the Bible say had no father?
A: Joshua, the son of Nun.

Q: What ailment killed Samson?
A: Fallen arches.

Q: How did Jonah's whale show charity?
A: Jonah was a stranger, and he took him in.

Q: How did Jonah feel after being swallowed by the whale?
A: Not too well. He was a little down in the mouth.

BISHOPS

* J O K E S *

How many bishops does it take to change a light bulb?
Only one, but the light bulb really has to want to change.

* * *

It was time for sacrament meeting to begin and a mother couldn't find her son. She searched all through the meetinghouse; then she looked outside. Finally she found him sitting on the curb with his head in his hands. "Son, we have to go in now," she said. "Church is about to start."

"I don't want to," he said.

"Why not?"

"Because nobody likes me. Nobody cares if I'm there or not. I'll bet you can't give me one good reason why I should."

"Oh, yes, I can," said the mother. "You're the bishop!"

* * *

One evening Bishop Limbergh was walking down the street to the chapel. On his way he saw little Tommy Taylor trying to reach the doorbell of a ward member's home. The bishop watched him for a moment, saw that the doorbell was too high, and went up to help him. "Hello, Tommy," the bishop said. He reached over the boy and pressed the doorbell for him. "There you go," the bishop said, "is that all you need?"

"Yeah, thanks," Tommy said. "And now we gotta run like heck!"

* * *

A Mormon bishop, a high priests group leader, and an elders quorum president were fishing from a boat in the middle of a small lake when the high priest realized he'd left his tackle box in the car. Not wanting to disturb the other two, he got out of the boat, walked over the water to the shore, got his gear, walked back, and started fishing.

An hour or so passed, and the bishop began to feel a little hungry. Unfortunately, he'd forgotten his lunch in the car. He excused himself, got out of the boat, walked over the water, got his lunch, came back, and nibbled on his sandwich.

The elders quorum president, not to be outdone, decided he'd go for a walk as well. He mumbled something about going to the bathroom, stood up, stepped over the side of the boat . . . and splashed into the lake.

The high priest, chuckling, said to the bishop, "Think we should've told him about the hidden stepping stones?"

The bishop raised his eyebrows in surprise. "What stepping stones?"

* * *

Question: How are bishops chosen?
Answer: The stake leaders find the most righteous, most spiritual, most loved person in the ward—and then they call her husband.

* QUOTATIONS *

Orson F. Whitney: I was a ward bishop for nearly twenty-eight years; and the highest compliment I ever received from our beloved President Joseph F. Smith, and about the only one, as a bishop, was when he told the people of my ward that there must be something to a man when they could "stomach him" for twenty-eight years as their bishop (Conference Report, Apr. 1917, 44).

BOOK OF MORMON

* QUOTATIONS *

Marion D. Hanks: I do not know whether I would be encouraged to say what I am going to quickly say to you now, but nobody is up here discouraging me, so I am going to do it. I have never heard anybody say there is anything very funny in the Book of Mormon but so far as I am concerned there is a lot of humor in it, because there are people involved. They are people like we are.

Here is one example. You all know that the book of Omni has five different writers. Now you are going to have to be alert to get this humor, but so far as I am concerned it is there. . . . Omni begins to write, then he passes the record on to his son, Amaron. After only a few verses Amaron writes, [then] passes them on to his brother Chemish. This is where I think there is something funny because it is about people. If any of you have ever kept records, or have been responsible for those who do, then this I think will find response in you.

"Now I, Chemish, write what few things I write, in the same book with my brother; for behold, I saw the last which he wrote, [Now he has had these records for years.] that he wrote it with his own hand; and he wrote it in the day that he delivered them unto me. [The next sentence immediately after is:] And after this manner we keep the records, . . . (Omni 1:9)" (*Speeches of the Year,* 4 May 1960, 6).

* S T O R I E S *

President George Albert Smith visited New York Governor Charles Whitman and presented him with a Book of Mormon; then later he visited the governor again during the time of World War I. "The conversation," President Smith later related, "turned to the war, and the governor was happily surprised at the number of LDS boys that I told him were in the services." The governor then asked President Smith, "But, how is this war coming out?"

"Don't you know, Governor?" President Smith asked.

"No," said the governor. "I don't know who is going to win it."

"Well," said President Smith, "where is your Book of Mormon?" The Church leader then read, "There shall be no kings upon this land. . . . I, the Lord, the God of heaven, will be their king." President Smith then explained that as long as the people of the United States of America keep the commandments, they will have the Lord's protection and watchcare.

"I had not seen that," said the governor.

President Smith replied, "You are not doing a very good job reading your Book of Mormon" (adapted from *Classic Stories from the Lives of Our Prophets*, 257).

BREVITY

* S T O R I E S *

A Washington socialite was sitting next to President Calvin Coolidge at a party.

"Oh, Mr. President," she said gushingly, "you are so silent. I made a bet today that I could get more than two words out of you."

"You lose," the president replied.

Callings

* JOKES *

A colonel on the governor's staff died suddenly, leaving many applicants clamoring for the position. Before the funeral, one of the most insistent managed to buttonhole the governor. "Don't you think I should take the colonel's place?" he asked.

"By all means," said the governor. "Speak to the undertaker."

* * *

Brother Hendricks, the ward choir director, took some time in priesthood meeting to try to increase enthusiasm for the choir. "We're going to be making personal calls to some of you, inviting you to join the choir," he said. "And we hope that you would be very diligent in these calls. Take your choir assignment as seriously as you do your home teaching."

To that, a young elder spoke up from the back, "Does that mean we only have to sing on the last day of each month?"

* QUOTATIONS *

Preston Nibley: When I received my release from the First Presidency, I did not know whether I wanted to come home or not, I felt so interested in my work. I remembered what my father told me about his mother when she was dying; she turned to him and said: "Charlie, this dying is no doings of mine" (Conference Report, Oct. 1940, 93).

* * *

J. Golden Kimball: A lot of people in the Church believe that men are called to leadership in the Church by revelation and some do not. But I'll tell you, when the Lord calls an old mule skinner like me to be a General Authority, there's got to be revelation (Cheney, *Golden Legacy*, 100).

* * *

Matthew Cowley, after being called to the Quorum of the Twelve Apostles: I have never sought, neither have I refused, any call that has ever come to me within the endowing power of the priesthood of God. I appeal also to you, to sustain me in this position. If I am sustained by you, the body of the Church, I am sure that I will be able to go about doing good. If you do not sustain me, heaven help me.

I sustain, here and now, the Authorities of this Church, from the highest unto the least. I have known President George Albert Smith all the days of my life. I have had the arms of his father about me in my childhood and in my early youth. I have had his arms about me in my maturity. I think it was he who set me apart for my first mission. He married me to my good wife. He took me upon my second mission— and now this! It seems that all the difficulties that have ever confronted me in life he is responsible for (Conference Report, Oct. 1945, 50).

* * *

Joseph Fielding Smith: My first Church assignment was to accompany Brigham Young to the dedication of the St. George Temple. Of course, I don't remember that assignment too well, for I was just one year old then (Joseph Fielding Smith, Jr., *Life of Joseph Fielding Smith*, 49).

* S T O R I E S *

In early 1968, President David O. McKay summoned [Hartman Rector, Jr., and his wife, Connie] to Salt Lake City for an interview. As they sat in the outer office wondering why the prophet of the Lord wanted to talk to a pair of converts from Missouri, they noticed a distinguished-looking young man and his wife also waiting to visit with President McKay. Through their nervousness, the Rectors noticed that their fellow sufferer was a lot taller than Hartman Rector—six and a half feet tall. They learned that his resumé was very impressive: he was first counselor in the New England Mission presidency and director of communications for the New England Council for Economic Development. They learned that his wife was Sharon Longden, a daughter of Elder John Longden, Assistant to the Twelve. His name was Loren C. Dunn. Finally Connie turned to Hartman and said with a smile, "If you two are interviewing for the same job, we'll be on the first plane home" (see Sessions, *Latter-day Patriots,* 184).

* * *

As president of the Church, Spencer W. Kimball once extended an assignment to two members of the Twelve. His counselor, N. Eldon Tanner, said, "I can't think of two finer men for this job."

One of them modestly replied, "Surely you can do better than us."

President Kimball countered, "Would you mind going ahead while we are looking for two better men?" (Kimball, "Spencer W. Kimball," *BYU Studies* 25[4]: 65).

* * *

Spencer W. Kimball loved to tell about an experience he had after being called as an apostle. In Arizona, where he was working to sell his business and his home, friends streamed into his office to offer congratulations and express their conviction of how right it was that he had been called. Then in came Evans Coleman, a cowpuncher type who had known Brother Kimball as a boy. He said, "So you're going to Salt Lake to be one of the Twelve Apostles, are you?"

"Yes, Evans, that's so."

"Well, it's clear that the Lord must have called you—because no one else would have thought of you!" (Kimball, "Spencer W. Kimball," *BYU Studies* 25[4]: 62).

CHARACTER

* J O K E S *

He who stands in the middle of the road is in a dangerous position; he gets knocked down by the traffic from both sides.

* Q U O T A T I O N S *

John Taylor: Jesus said, My sheep hear my voice, and they know me, and a stranger they will not follow, because they know not the voice of a stranger. And why do not the millions of the inhabitants of the earth embrace the Gospel? Because they are not sheep; that is all. And if the goats kick up and cut a few antics, you need not be astonished. It is the nature of goats, is it not? (*Journal of Discourses* 22:305).

* STORIES *

Campaigning in Brooklyn in 1940, Franklin Delano Roosevelt made this humorous reference to those who "change colors" and whose loyalty is uncertain: "We all know the story of the unfortunate chameleon which turned brown when placed on a brown rug, and turned red when placed on a red rug, but who died a tragic death when they put him on a Scotch plaid."

* * *

Late in the life of Church President Harold B. Lee, a film crew tried to convince him to wear makeup for the filming of his Christmas message. President Lee was not willing to comply even though he looked rather tired and pale. "All important people have to wear makeup for filming," one of the film crew said. "For instance, President Eisenhower used to have makeup put on him and President Nixon has found he needs to wear it for television appearances.

"Yes," President Lee answered with a smile, "but I'm not running for office" (see *This People*, Aug./Sept. 1985, 53).

CHARITY

* JOKES *

A trainee police officer was asked, "How would you go about breaking up a crowd?"
His answer: "Take up a collection. That'll do it every time."

* STORIES *

Thackeray told of an Irishwoman begging alms from him, who, when she saw him put his hand in his pocket, cried out:

"May the blessing of God follow ye all yer life!" But when he only pulled out his snuff box, she immediately added: "and never overtake ye."

CHASTENING

* STORIES *

Once when J. Golden Kimball was attending a conference in southern Utah, he proclaimed to the members, "If you don't mend your ways only ten percent of you are going to make the celestial kingdom!" The people were outraged, and they wrote a letter of protest to the First Presidency. The next conference, the First Presidency sent Brother Kimball back to the same area with instructions to apologize to the people.

When it was Elder Kimball's turn to speak, he stood and said, "I have been sent here to apologize for a statement I made a few months ago. After looking things over again and with careful thought and much prayer, I will have to apologize for my rash remark. If you don't mend your ways, only five percent of you will make it to the celestial kingdom, not a d—— bit more!" (Cheney, *Golden Legacy*, 47–48).

CHILDREN

* J O K E S *

Primary teacher: So your mother says prayers with you every night? What does she say?

Little boy: Thank heavens, he's in bed!

* * *

A young mother put her little Jacob in bed for the night, but he toddled after her down the hall. "No, Jacob," she said. "You have to stay in bed."

She put him back in bed, turned off the light, and started to leave. "Mommy, Mommy!" Jacob called.

"What do you want?"

"Uh—how many days before Christmas?"

"Three months," she said. "Now go to sleep."

She walked down the hall again. "Mommy, Mommy!" he called.

"What?"

"Can I play with Todd tomorrow?"

"We'll see."

Again: "Mommy, Mommy."

"Jacob, this is the last time. What do you want?"

"Uh—where's Daddy?"

"He's at a meeting. Now if you yell 'Mommy' again you'll be in real trouble."

She was almost to the end of the hall when he called again: "Sister Green! Sister Green! May I have a drink of water?"

* * *

When a bishop telephoned one of the families in the ward, their little girl answered. "My parents are busy," she said politely. "May I take a message?"

"This is the bishop."

"How do you spell *bishop?*"

The bishop spelled out the word, then waited.

"How do you make a B?"

* * *

Lance, age four, was very cross at the supper table.

"The trouble with you is," said his mother, "you didn't take a nap this afternoon."

Lance looked at his mother directly and said, "Yes, and what's your trouble?"

* * *

It was Kindness to Animals Week at school, and a fourth grader came home full of pride. His parents asked him why he was so happy, and he told them that each student had to do something special for the week and that what he did had really worked.

"And what did you do?" asked his mother.

"I kicked a boy for kicking his dog."

* * *

Two men were catching up at a missionary reunion.

"I have three children now," one of them said.

"I sure wish I had three children."

"Don't you have children yet?"

"Yes, six!"

* * *

The tornado touched down, uprooted a tree in the family's front yard, and completely demolished the house across the street. The father went to the door, glanced out, and muttered, "Darn kids!" Then he went back to reading the paper.

* * *

The best years of a parent's life are when the kids are old enough to mow lawns and shovel snow but too young to drive the car.

* * *

On the way home from church, little Ethan asked his mother, "Are we really made of dust?"

"Yes, we are," she answered.

"Do we really return to dust again when we die?"

"Yes, that's what the scriptures say."

"Well, Mom," said Ethan, "Last night when I said my prayers, I looked under my bed, and somebody under there is either coming or going."

* * *

Recently there were tremors in a California town, and the townspeople got nervous. One couple sent their little boy to stay with an aunt and uncle in another town, explaining that the impending earthquake was the reason for the visit.

A few days later the parents got a short letter: "We're returning your boy. Send the earthquake."

* * *

Aunt Barbara: Does your baby sister talk yet, Susan?

Susan: No, she doesn't have to. She gets everything she wants just by howling and yelling.

* * *

First little boy: Hi, my name is Billy. I'm five. How old are you?

Second little boy: I'm Tommy, but I don't know how old I am.

First little boy: Do girls drive you crazy?

Second little boy: Nope.
First little boy: Okay. You're four then.

* * *

After reading the parable of the prodigal son, the Primary teacher wanted the class to understand the feelings of the prodigal's elder brother. She said, "During the rejoicing, there was someone who felt no joy; among the happy people, there was one who felt only bitterness; among all those going to the feast, there was one who had no wish to attend. Who do you think this was?" After several moments of silence a child replied, "The fatted calf?"

* * *

A new baby wailed in his crib while his five-year-old sister tried to comfort him.
"Are you sure he came from heaven?" she asked her mother.
"Yes, dear," her mother replied.
"No wonder they sent him down here!"

* * *

The Primary was holding a party to teach the older children to dance. One of the teachers watched beamingly as she helped a ten-year-old boy ask a girl for a dance. Half an hour later, the boy asked, "Now how do I get rid of her?"

* * *

A home teacher called to make an appointment. The phone rang and the family's little boy answered in a whisper. "Hello."
Home teacher: Is your daddy there?
Boy (whisper): Yes.
Home teacher: Can I speak with him?
Boy (whisper): He's busy.
Home teacher: Is your mommy there?
Boy (whisper): Yes.

Home teacher: Can I speak with her?

Boy (whisper): She's busy.

Home teacher: Is there anyone else there I could talk to?

Boy (whisper): The fire department.

Home teacher: The fire department!

Boy: (whisper) Yes, they're busy too.

Home teacher: Is there anybody *else* there?

Boy (whisper): The police department.

Home teacher: What, them too?

Boy (whisper): Yep. But they're busy.

Home teacher: Let me get this straight: your mother, your father, the fire department, *and* the police department are *all* in your house and they're *all* busy. What's going on over there?

Boy (whisper): Everyone's looking for me.

* * *

Little Justin was saying his prayers one night, and as his mother tiptoed near his bedroom door, she heard him say, "Please bless Jeremy that he'll stop hitting me. You might remember that I've mentioned this before. Well, he's still doing it."

* * *

A little girl complained that she didn't want to go back to school. "But why, Jenny?" asked her mother.

"Well, I can't read, I can't write, and they won't let me talk."

* * *

Primary teacher: Billy, what do you think a land flowing with milk and honey would be like?

Billy: Sticky!

* QUOTATIONS *

Jedediah M. Grant: Brother Brigham is a father to the Quorums of this Church; and when the people are right, has he a disposition to chastise them? No, he has a fatherly feeling to bless them, and so has brother Heber. I do not know whether I have as much of that feeling as either of them, with regard to the Church, but I do not suppose that there is a man on the earth that is fonder of children than I am. If I do not like old people so well as some do, I like children well enough to balance the deficiency (*Journal of Discourses* 4:86).

* * *

Orson F. Whitney: I am reminded of another story, told by the famous temperance orator, John B. Gough, in a lecture delivered at the Salt Lake Theater many years ago. He was deprecating the practice of simplifying the Bible for the study of children. "Children," said he, "understand much better than we give them credit for. Let them read the Bible just as it is; they will understand it." To illustrate the point, he told of two little boys, Johnny and Billy, who were engaged in conversation. Johnny was seated on his mother's door-step, whittling a stick, and Billy had just caught a fly. He came with it to Johnny, and said: "What a funny thing a fly is. See what lots of legs he's got: and every time I blow him he buzzes." Then he would blow on the fly, and hold it up to his ear, to hear it buzz, grinning with delight at the sound. Finally he remarked, "I wonder how God made him." And the great orator paused long enough to observe, "Many a learned man has asked the same question, and could not answer it." But Johnny had an idea of how God made the fly. "Well, Billy," said he, as he whittled away. "God don't make flies like men make houses. When He wants flies, he says, Let there be flies: and then there is flies" (Conference Report, Apr. 1911, 50).

* * *

Hugh B. Brown: An influence on my upbringing was my older brother Bud. One day Bud and I saw a weasel. The little animal ran into his hole, and we got a spade and began to dig him out. We dug down quite a ways, and Bud said, "I think I can hear him down there, we are pretty close to him. Maybe you'd better reach in and see what he's doing." I rolled up my sleeve and reached down into the hole. Well, the weasel got me by the finger, and I still have a scar.

On another occasion, Bud and I went out to the barn, where he helped me up until I could get ahold of the rafters across the top with my hands. Bud said, "I will swing you back and forth. When you get going pretty good, I will tell you when to let loose of that rafter and when to grab the next one." He gave me a good long swing and then said, "Now." I let loose of the rafter, but the other one was not within reach. It took me six hours to wake up as I landed on the back of my head. Needless to say, mother was very concerned for my welfare.

So things went on between Bud and me. But I never felt any animosity or ill-will towards him. It seemed to be part of my education, although he certainly had me in trouble most of the time. But the time soon came when I wanted to get even with Bud for all of his mischief. I had read a story in which a man died, was put in a big vault, and then came to life again. He got out of his casket in the night and walked around, trying to find his way out, but he kept placing his hands on the faces of the other dead men around him. It was a terrible, horrifying story. I knew if I could get Bud to read it he would react as I had. So I asked him to read it. As he read and marked the book I watched him carefully. When he got to the place where the man was walking around among the dead men, Bud was very excited, to say the least.

At the time, we slept on some hay in the basement of a big barn at Lake Breeze (where my father managed a fourteen-acre orchard between North Temple and 200 South streets on Redwood Road). When Bud got to this place in the book, I said, "Leave your book now and we'll go to bed." He put it down reluctantly and we went out to the barn. I pulled the barn door open. Inside was as dark as a stack of black cats. I had previously arranged for a cousin to be in the basement in a sheet. When we opened the door and he saw this ghost standing at the bottom of the steps, Bud gave an unearthly scream and started to run. I overtook him and brought him back. "That's just the result of the book you've been reading," I said. "Don't be so foolish. I'll show you there's no ghost there." I went down the steps, felt all around, and could not feel the ghost.

Bud decided to trust me. He went down, got into bed, and covered up his head, but he was shaking all over. I said, "Don't be so foolish, Bud. Uncover your head and look around you. You'll see that there are no ghosts here." He uncovered his head and the ghost was standing right at the foot of his bed. He let out another unearthly scream, covered his head again, and began to pray. I felt very guilty because he told the Lord all the bad things he had done and promised never to do any more. Finally, the ghost went away. I guess Bud's prayer had a great effect on him, as well (Firmage, *An Abundant Life,* 2–4).

* STORIES *

During gold rush days in California, a woman took her infant to the theatre one evening and it started crying just as the orchestra began to play.

"Stop those fiddles and let the baby cry," called a man in the pit. "I haven't heard such a sound in ten years!"

The audience applauded the sentiment wildly, the orchestra was stopped, and the baby continued its performance amid unbounded enthusiasm.

* * *

Once a kindergarten teacher was helping her young student put on his galoshes. They seemed far too small. She pushed and tugged and pulled and stretched the boot until she finally got it on. Then she went through the whole procedure for the other boot. She was tired and sweaty but satisfied when she was done. "There you go, Billy," she said. "You're all set."

"These are not my galoshes," he said.

"Oh, my word," the teacher said. She yanked and pulled and struggled and finally got both boots off again.

"They're my sister's," he explained, "but my mother made me wear them today" (adapted from Conference Report, Oct. 1987, 31).

* * *

A little girl once asked Herbert Hoover, president of the United States from 1929 to 1933, what he had enjoyed most about his presidential years. President Hoover replied, "The thing I enjoyed most was visits from children. They did not want public offices."

* * *

Not long after [Harold B.] Lee was sustained as the president of the Church, he received a note from a Primary president with a touching story: "I held up your picture and said to the children that this was our new president of the Church, Harold B. Lee. A little hand shot up quickly. 'Oh, I know him,' said the little boy. 'We sing about him all the time in church: Reverent-lee, quiet-lee . . .'" (Swinton, *In the Company of Prophets*, 72–73).

CHRISTMAS

* J O K E S *

The three stages of life: You believe in Santa Claus, you don't believe in Santa Claus, you are Santa Claus.

* Q U O T A T I O N S *

Elaine Jack: Much as I love fragrant, green trees, I followed the fashion in the early sixties and decided to flock our tree. I thought the natural look of a tree after a snowstorm would be a wonderful addition to our Christmas decor. With a do-it-yourself flocking kit that attached to my vacuum cleaner, I was sure I could create a beautiful tree for much less than a tree cost on a lot. I decided that I would do the job right where the tree would stand so none of the flocking would be disturbed. I connected the vacuum to the powdery flocking material and the bottle of water and turned on the power. It worked! Synthetic snow made the tree look like a winter wonderland. As I finished and stepped back to admire my Currier and Ives tree, I noticed that the wall, the sofa, the piano, and the chairs were also part of my winter wonderland. We had a spectacular tree, but snow removal that year continued into June (Jack, *Eye to Eye, Heart to Heart*, 172).

CHURCH ACTIVITY

* JOKES *

Bishop Jones to a prospective missionary: Rob, the Church needs you. It's time for you to join the army of the Lord.

Rob: I'm already in the army of the Lord, Bishop.

Bishop Jones: What do you mean? You hardly even come to Church.

Rob (whispering): Well, you see, I'm in the Secret Service.

* POEMS *

Each time I pass a church,
I always pay a visit,
So when at last I'm carried in,
The Lord won't say, "Who is it?"

COMMANDMENTS

* JOKES *

A woman went to the post office to mail her daughter a new set of scriptures. The clerk asked if the package contained anything breakable. "Just the Ten Commandments," she replied.

* STORIES *

A newspaper editor who needed to fill some space ran the Ten Commandments without comment. A few days later he heard from an angry subscriber: "Cancel my subscription. You're getting too personal."

COMMUNICATION

* JOKES *

A man walked into a doctor's office. The receptionist asked him, "What do you have?"

"Shingles," the man answered.

The receptionist gave him a long medical form to fill out. A nurse walked by and asked him, "What do you have?"

"Shingles," he answered again.

The nurse sent him back to the examination room, and the doctor appeared and asked, "What do you have?"

"Shingles!" the man practically yelled.

"Where?" asked the doctor.

"For heaven's sake! They're out in the truck! Where do you want me to put them?"

* * *

The chapel was full to overflowing. Shortly after the meeting started the bishop noticed that the stake presidency had made a surprise visit and were standing by the back door. Since there were no

47

empty seats on the stand, he leaned forward and whispered to one of the deacons on the front row: "Jimmy, please get me three chairs."

Jimmy, an athletic little lad who was willing to do almost anything for the bishop, couldn't quite hear what the bishop had said. So he replied, "What?" in a rather loud whisper. The bishop whispered back, "Get me three chairs."

Jimmy, a bit confused, looked at the bishop and asked again, "What?" Again the bishop said, "Get me three chairs." Jimmy smiled, leaned back, and winked at the bishop. The bishop, a little puzzled, looked at Jimmy. "Did you understand what I said?" he asked. Jimmy smiled, winked again, and nodded his head. "Well, then do it now!" the bishop said with some exasperation.

Jimmy looked at the bishop. "Now? Well, okay . . ." Then he shrugged his shoulders, jumped to his feet, and yelled, "Rah, rah, rah, Bishop!" (see *A Time to Laugh*, 51–52).

* * *

A ward had some money left over at the end of the year, and the ward council was discussing how to spend it.

"I think we need new scriptures for the library," one member said.

"How about replanting the flowers outside," suggested another. "They're looking pretty dingy."

"Those are good suggestions," the bishop said, "but what I'd really like to see is a nice chandelier in the west foyer."

Before he could put it to a vote, however, the ward clerk raised his hand. "With all due respect, Bishop, I think we should do something else. In the first place, no one here knows how to spell it, so I don't know how to order it. In the second place, I doubt the foyer is big enough for any chandelier. In the third place, there's not a single soul in the whole ward who will know how to play it. And finally, Bishop, what we really need in that foyer is some lights!"

* * *

City cousin: Look at that bunch of cows.

Country cousin: Don't you know anything? Not bunch. Herd.

City cousin: Heard what?

Country cousin: Herd of cows.

City cousin: Of course I've heard of cows! How stupid do you think I am?

Country cousin: No! A cow herd.

City cousin: Why should I care if a cow heard? I've got no secrets from a cow!

* * *

A farmer had a wife who was very critical of his vocabulary. One evening he told her he had a friend named Bill he would like for her to meet. "Don't call him 'Bill,'" she insisted. "Call him 'William.'"

When the friend arrived, the farmer said, "Let me tell you a tale."

"Not tale," the wife interrupted. "Say 'anecdote.'"

That night, upon retiring, the farmer told her to put out the light.

"Not 'put out,'" she exclaimed. "Say 'extinguish' the light."

Later in the night she awakened her husband and sent him downstairs to investigate a noise. When he returned, she asked him what it was.

"It was," he explained carefully, "a William goat which I took by its anecdote and extinguished."

* * *

"When my husband was on his death bed," Sister Heltzer explained to her friends, "he told me he had three envelopes in his desk drawer. He said they would take care of everything.

"Not long after he died, I got out the envelopes. The first one said 'For the casket.' It had $5,000 in it, and I used it to buy a nice casket. The second envelope said, 'For the expenses.' It had $4,000 in it, which was just enough to take care of the other bills from the funeral.

The last envelope said 'For the stone.' It had $3,000 in it. And look!"
she exclaimed, holding her hand out to her friends, fingers extended,
"isn't it beautiful!"

* * *

A family was eating dinner.
Son: Dad, is it okay to eat caterpillars?
Dad: Billy! You know better than to talk like that at the table.
Son: Sorry. It's just that a minute ago there was one on your salad.
But it's gone now.

* * *

A son went to ask his father for money. Their conversation went
like this:
Father: I'm busy. Be short.
Son: I will. I am.

* * *

"How is your wife?" one man asked another.
"She is in heaven," replied the friend.
"Oh, I'm sorry," stammered the man. Then he realized this was
not the thing to say. "I mean," he stammered, "I'm glad." That seemed
even worse so he blurted, "Well, what I really mean is, I'm surprised."

* * *

A customer settled himself and let the barber put a towel around
him. Then he told the barber, "Before we start, I know the weather's
awful. I don't care who wins the next big fight, and I don't bet on the
horse races. I know I'm getting thin on top, but I don't mind. Now
get on with it."
"Well, sir, if you don't mind," said the barber, "I'll be able to concentrate better if you don't talk so much!"

* * *

Brother Blicker came home from work with a joke to tell his wife. "Did you hear the one about the window that needed cleaning?" he asked.

"No, I don't believe I have," she answered.

"Well, I guess I shouldn't tell you—you couldn't see through it anyway."

Sister Blicker thought that was pretty clever. When she went visiting teaching she said, "Have you heard the story about the window you couldn't see through?"

"No, tell me," the sister answered.

"Oh, I'd better not," Sister Blicker said. "It's too dirty to tell" (see Brown, *BYU Speeches of the Year,* 16 Feb. 1954, 1–2).

∗ Q U O T A T I O N S ∗

Orson Hyde apparently sometimes had trouble with people misspelling and mispronouncing his name—particularly in England, where the custom was to drop the "H" at the beginning of a word. To clarify matters, Elder Hyde put the following notice in the *Millennial Star:*

"Persons procuring post-office orders to send us are requested to be particular in giving our name correctly. Some orders have come payable to 'Horse and Hide,' some to 'Horson Ide.' . . . Remember that our name is—ORSON HYDE" (quoted in Taylor, *Kingdom or Nothing,* 121).

∗ ∗ ∗

Jacob de Jager: A friend taught me a lot about ballooning. . . . I also heard from my friend many delightful stories about previous balloon flights. On one occasion, as the story goes, clouds developed unexpectedly during a flight, and the two men in the wicker basket had not the faintest idea over which part of the country they were sailing.

They decided to lower the balloon, and all of a sudden they saw a Dutchman walking on a lonely country road. When they were able to draw his attention, one of the men in the basket shouted: "Where are we?" And the lonely walker looked up, cupped his hands around his mouth, and shouted back, "You are in a balloon."

To make their urgent request for direction more clear, the man in the balloon cried vigorously, "Where are *you?*" And the man called back at the top of his voice, "I am on the ground!" (*Ensign*, May 1983, 75).

* STORIES *

The late General Smedley D. Butler, always an impulsive man, was generally careful of the welfare of his men. One time in France he encountered two soldiers emerging from the kitchen with a large soup kettle. "Let me taste that," he ordered.

"But Gen— . . ."

"No buts! Give me a spoon." Taking a taste, the General sputtered, "You don't call that soup, do you?"

"No, sir," replied the soldier, "I was trying to tell you, sir, I call that dishwater."

* * *

Once, when Abraham Lincoln's secretary of state suggested that a message Lincoln was sending to the British prime minister be put in more diplomatic terms because of the prime minister's high position, Lincoln said, "Mr. Secretary, do you suppose Palmerston will understand our position from my letter, just as it is?"

"Certainly, Mr. President."

"Do you suppose the London *Times* will?"

"Certainly."

"Do you suppose the average Englishman of affairs will?"

"Certainly. It cannot be mistaken in England."

"Do you suppose that a hackman on his box will understand it?"

"Very readily, Mr. President."

"Very well, Mr. Secretary. I guess we'll let her slide just as she is."

* * *

A melancholy man, always quoting death statistics, once accosted Mark Twain, commenting, "Mr. Clemens, do you realize that every time I breathe, an immortal soul passes into eternity?"

Twain asked sweetly, "Have you ever tried cloves?"

* * *

Camilla Kimball's deaf sister stayed with the Kimballs for twenty-five years. After her death, Elder Kimball's son Ed, meaning to be helpful, asked him, "Do you want me to call [my brothers] Andy and Spencer to tell them about Aunt Mary's death?"

"Yes," he replied, "would you please."

"Would you like me to call one of them before the other?"

Elder Kimball paused. "Yes" (Kimball, "Spencer W. Kimball," *BYU Studies* 25[4]: 68).

* * *

Back when bishops were responsible to raise budget money from ward members, a ward had a project of selling bags of lawn fertilizer. The bishop, who was quite hard of hearing, stood at the pulpit and made the announcement, then sat down.

His counselor stood to conduct the meeting. "We want to remind you that next week is fast Sunday. We've noticed that we have quite a few new mothers, with babies to be blessed, so remember that next week is the time."

At that the hard-of-hearing bishop, who thought the counselor was still talking about fertilizer, piped up from behind him. "And don't forget that if you haven't got yours yet I can get them for five bucks apiece!"

COMPLAINING

* JOKES *

A special group of monks was able to utter only two words every ten years. After the first ten years, Brother Francis said to his superior: "Bed hard."

After the twentieth year, he said to the same superior: "Food cold."

Finally, after the thirtieth year, he said to the same superior: "I quit."

The superior responded: "I'm not surprised. All you've done in thirty years is complain, complain, complain!"

COMPLIMENTS

* QUOTATIONS *

George A. Smith: It puts me in mind of a compliment paid to Queen Elizabeth by an English farmer. Her Majesty was out on a ride, and was caught in a storm. The farmer was very much rejoiced that the Queen had called upon him, and she was pleased with his rough hospitality. Being just after the defeat of the Spanish Armada, he complimented her on the success of her arms by saying—"The King of Spain got the wrong sow by the ear when he made war with your Majesty." The Queen was much amused at this vulgar comparison (*Journal of Discourses* 8:254–55).

COMPROMISE

* JOKES *

After a long private meeting, two politicians came out to face some eager reporters. One reporter asked, "Was the meeting a success?"

"Yes," replied one of the politicians. "We had an excellent exchange of views."

"What do you mean, an exchange of views?" asked the reporter.

"Well, I'll explain," said the politician. "He came in with his views and went out with mine."

CONSCIENCE

* JOKES *

Did you hear about the man who refused to listen to his conscience? He didn't want to take advice from a total stranger.

CONTENTION

Nine-year-old Travis came home from school with a black eye and a bloody nose.

Dad: You look terrible! What happened?

Travis: I challenged Jeremy to a duel, and he got to choose his weapon.

Dad: Well, that seems fair.

Travis: Yeah, but I didn't know he'd choose his sister!

* * *

Dad: Shawn, what did you do when Erik called you a liar?

Shawn: Well, Dad, I remembered what you taught me about a soft answer turning away anger.

Dad: That's wonderful! What did you say to him?

Shawn: Well . . . I answered him with a soft tomato.

J. Golden Kimball: Educated as we are, and breathing this mountain air for twenty years, it takes a little training before you can turn the other cheek and treat those kindly who spitefully use you. It takes a little education to learn how precious are the souls of the children of men in the sight of God. So we need some older men to put their hands on us younger boys and hold us down. We are a good deal like Peter. I was that way. I would have cut more than one of their ears off, if there had been someone to stick them on again (Conference Report, Apr. 1902, 9).

* * *

B. H. Roberts: I really never had, in my boyhood days, a fight in my life but what it was forced on me. . . . Personally I was just in the same condition that the nations of Europe are now in, I was forced to fight; and generally, in fact so far as I can remember always, I entered every engagement that fell in my way with a good deal of anxiety, even fear, but there was this peculiarity about it—I don't know that it is peculiar, however; perhaps it is a common inheritance to all men— but the first blow struck, I was always very comfortable after that (Conference Report, Oct. 1914, 108).

* * *

Hugh B. Brown: A middle-aged couple on the farm had a violent quarrel at breakfast time. Later in the day they started for town in the buggy, with a fine team of horses to sell their vegetables and eggs. As the horses trotted along, Mary said, "John, why can't we travel together like these horses do? They don't quarrel and fight." John said, "Mary, we could if there was only one tongue between us" (Conference Report, Oct. 1954, 16).

COOPERATION

* QUOTATIONS *

Robert E. Wells: When we fake our efforts, we tend to have a negative effect on the project at hand. I often think of the story of two missionaries on a bicycle built for two. They were going up a steep hill. It was a difficult climb, and at the top the two stopped to rest.

The young missionary up front, dripping with perspiration, remarked, "Boy, that was a steep hill. I didn't think we'd make it."

The other companion, with total composure, looked down the steep grade and said, "I'm sure we'd have gone backwards if I hadn't had the brake on all the way up" (*New Era*, April 1977, 6).

COURAGE

* **S T O R I E S** *

A Confederate soldier was seen by General Lee, who met him retiring from the front with what Lee considered unbecoming haste. Lee said to him, "Why don't you go back to the front? That's the place where a soldier should be when a battle is going on."

The reply was, "General, I have been there, and I give you my word of honor it is not a place where any self-respecting man would care to be."

* * *

One day Chauncey Depew met a Civil War soldier who had been wounded in the face. He was a Union man, and Depew asked him in which battle he had been injured.

"In the last battle of Bull Run, sir," he replied. "But how could you get hit in the face at Bull Run?" "Well, sir," said the man, half apologetically, "after I had run a mile or two I got careless and looked back."

Courtesy

* QUOTATIONS *

David O. McKay: Yesterday morning when our President suggested to this vast assemblage that they move nearer together in their seats, in order to give brethren and sisters who were standing a little room to sit down, there was a universal movement throughout this tabernacle. It was surprising to those who could look over the audience, to see how just a little one-sixteenth of an inch, multiplied by probably ten thousand, made room for so many people. There was a universal response to that suggestion. Some were unable to give even the sixteenth of an inch, but they wiggled all the same (Conference Report, Oct. 1909, 88).

* * *

George Albert Smith: You have done such fine teamwork during the day, brethren, you have collapsed sufficiently two or three times, by moving closer together so that many people who were standing could have seats. I am going to ask you if you will do that tonight, if you will all move to the center of the seats. And when I say move to the center, I do not mean just to go through the motion, I mean move (Conference Report, Apr. 1946, 103).

* * *

Cornelius Zappey (former president of the Netherlands Mission): Six months ago, my brothers and sisters, I was standing in the aisle, behind the rope held by the usher, wishing, as many of us have done, that all Stake Presidents and Bishops would not be on time. Standing in the end of the row two sisters behind me were speaking the Scandinavian language. It did not take long before they were in front of me, and in some way, soon they were at the very front but while

59

they were yet in front of me speaking their native tongue, a brother in front of them turned around and asked: "Swensk?" and the sisters said "Ja, Ja." This brother, putting his hand upon his chest said, "Norsk." It did not take long until the sisters were in front of this brother also. . . . I never before understood better and more fully the statement that "The race is not to the swift but to the one that endureth to the end" than I did at that time (Conference Report, Apr. 1951, 132–33).

* * *

George Albert Smith: It is evident that we have more people in the building this morning than we had yesterday. We will appreciate it if those who are comfortably seated now will take a little less space, crowd toward the center of the benches, and I think we can probably make room for most of those who are now standing. There are probably 150 or 200 standing. We will ask the ushers to bring you to your places. I would like to suggest that there is room for twelve or fifteen people on the steps of the stand here, and for the information of those of you who are in the habit of sitting on the stand, I should like to suggest that that is where I sat a few years ago because there wasn't any place that I could see that somebody else did not have. I sat on the steps of the stand and before that Conference was finished, I was sustained as a member of the Quorum of the Twelve. . . . We shall all be happier if everybody can be seated, and I am sure you are making good progress, and I thank you for it (Conference Report, Apr. 1946, 55).

CREATION

* STORIES *

The noted agnostic Colonel Robert Ingersoll, during a visit with the famous preacher Henry Ward Beecher, noted a beautiful globe portraying the constellations and stars of the heavens. "This is just what I've been looking for," he said after examining it. "Who made it?"

"Who made it?" repeated Beecher in simulated astonishment. "Why Colonel, nobody made it; it just happened."

CREATIVITY

* QUOTATIONS *

William J. Critchlow, Jr.: This mother skunk had twin babies. They gave her a lot of trouble. She named one of them IN—and the other she named OUT. Now it seemed that whenever IN was in—OUT was out, and when OUT was in, IN was out. One day she called OUT in and said to him, "OUT, go out in the forest and find IN and bring IN in." So OUT went out in the forest and found IN and brought IN in. "Wonderful," said the mother. "How did you do it?" "It was easy," said OUT. "Instinct" (*Speeches of the Year,* 28 Apr. 1964, 6).

* * *

Moses W. Taylor: We believe in temperance. Some of the Saints in our stake will hardly drink hot water, and some almost hesitate to use hot gravy. . . . Let me tell you what one of the bishops of one of our wards did, and the Relief Society helped him in it. There was a saloon started in the ward, and made us all kinds of trouble. Some time passed, and the members of the Church bought a lot just opposite the saloon on which to build a meeting house. Then the bishop came to the presidency of the stake and said, "What shall we do about that saloon?" The presidency of the stake said, you go on hauling and cutting rock every day, right along. So they did it, and in about three weeks, he telephoned the presidency of the stake, and said, This saloon man has got quite friendly, he comes out, and talks with me. The people don't patronize him very much, and he says he will sell his saloon for so much, what shall we do? I told him to offer $50 less, and I will give you the money. Then the Relief Society bought it; and the women went into the vacated saloon, and they got lime and made it into whitewash, and they whitewashed floors and everything else nearly; they wanted to wash the sin away, you know. And then they erected a long board table in it, and every day they got up a big dinner in that old saloon building. Now they have got as fine a meeting house right opposite that former saloon building as there is any where, and the people built it, and it didn't cost them very much money. Thus sometimes you see, a saloon building is a very nice thing to have, if it is used by the Relief Society (Conference Report, Apr. 1908, 65–66).

CURIOSITY

* **JOKES** *

Grade school teacher (giving lesson about Ben Franklin and electricity): So you see, Mr. Franklin's curiosity was a good thing. He discovered electricity. Now, where would we be if no one had ever been curious?

Student: In the Garden of Eden!

DATING AND COURTSHIP

* JOKES *

Amy: I'm engaged! Look, he gave me a diamond ring!

Tiffany: How nice. I'm glad to see you're marrying a thrifty man.

* * *

College student to date at a basketball game: Look at that tall player who just made the hook shot. He'll be our best man before the season's finished.

Date: Sweetheart! What a creative way to ask me to marry you!

* * *

She said: The man of my dreams is as brave as a lion, as handsome as a movie star, but still humble. He's as smart as a whip, as wise as Solomon, as strong as Samson but as gentle as a lamb. He's kind to all women but loves only me.

He said: How lucky we met!

* * *

He said: You're the sunshine of my life. When you're near me, the gray clouds disappear and the radiant beams of light chase away the dark and the cold. When you leave me, the world is chilly and the clouds appear . . .

She said: Is this a marriage proposal or a weather report?

* * *

Chad: I think my girlfriend is taking advantage of me.

Zach: What makes you say that?

Chad: The other night when I invited her out to dinner, she asked if she could bring a date.

* * *

John: Will you marry me?

Marsha: No, dear, but I'll always admire your excellent taste.

* * *

Boy, with one hand cupped over the other: If you can guess what I have in my hand, I'll take you out tonight.

Girl: An elephant!

Boy: Nope! But that's close enough. I'll pick you up at 7:30.

* * *

He said: Do you love me?

She said: Yes, you know I do.

He said: Would you be willing to live on my income?

She said: Of course. That is—if you can get another one for yourself.

* * *

Chaz: So . . . how did it go when you asked that good-looking girl to dance?

Brett: Not bad, really.

Chaz: Yeah? She gave you some encouragement, then?

Brett: Well, she looked at me twice before saying no.

* * *

Boy: Meet me at La Caille at seven o'clock tonight.

Girl: La Caille? Wow! That's a really classy restaurant!

Boy: Yeah. And besides, it's really close to the hamburger joint where we're going to eat.

* * *

Dad: Well, Son, I'll bet you feel pretty grown-up now that you've turned sixteen and gone on your first date!

Todd: I'd feel a lot more grown-up if Mom hadn't taken pictures and recorded it in my baby book!

* * *

A single man was visiting a new ward and saw only one empty seat—between two attractive ladies. He felt timid about taking that spot and held back at the doorway. The greeter, a fatherly type, saw him hesitating and said encouragingly, "You go on in and sit down. They won't mind."

The fellow gulped. "But what would I say to them?"

"Just be friendly," the older man suggested. "Ask them if they're married and if they have any children."

He nervously sat down between the two ladies, turned to the one on the right, and asked, "Do you have children?"

"Yes," she replied.

"Are you married?" She glared at him; then turned away.

Hoping for better results with the other lady, he turned to her and asked, "Are you married?"

"No," she answered.

"Do you have any children?"

* * *

Susan: Don't worry, darling. I love you so much I'm willing to share all your troubles.

Sam: But, baby, I don't even *have* any troubles.

Susan: I don't mean now—I'm talking about *after* we're married.

* * *

Every time a certain young woman went to Church, she'd walk up to the men and give them a big kiss. Finally the bishop told her she'd have to stop. "I'm just following the scripture," she said.

"What scripture is that?" the bishop asked.

"Matthew 7:12: 'All things whatsoever ye would that men should do to you, do ye even so to them.'"

Later, the bishop also counseled her about dancing too close with all of the men at a ward social. She replied, "1 Thessalonians 5:21: 'Prove all things; hold fast that which is good.'"

* * *

One young woman who dated a lot was distraught because none of her boyfriends wanted to get married. "They draw near unto me with their lips," she said, "but their hearts are far from me."

* * *

Karen: I understand John has finally asked you to marry him. Did he mention that he once proposed to me?

Kristin: Not specifically. But he did say he'd done a lot of foolish things before he met me.

* QUOTATIONS *

Clarissa Young, one of Brigham Young's daughters: On Sunday evenings the older girls were permitted to entertain their beaux in the parlor. The oldest members of the group became rather famous as the "Big Ten," because there were just that number who seemed to have grown up about the same time. There was only the one large parlor for them to entertain their young men in, and twenty did seem a large number when there were only four corners, so, one evening, the happy suggestion was made that some semblance of privacy might be obtained by turning down the coal-oil lamp that stood on the table in the center of the room. A second thought was that the light might be more effectively dimmed by placing a barricade of books around it. The main idea, anyway, was to get rid of the light, so everyone lent a hand, and soon there was but one shaft of light that played upon the ceiling where no one minded it. The couples then went back to their chairs and the sofa, which seemed so much more cozy in the semidarkness.

All went very well for a time until the door slowly opened, and there stood Father with a candle in his hand. He gave one look around the room and then walked to the table where he removed the books one by one until the proper light shone forth on faces that would have preferred the darkness for a different reason now. Then turning to the very much subdued group, he said, "The girls will go upstairs to their rooms, and I will say good night to the young men" (Spencer, *Brigham Young at Home,* 33–34).

* S T O R I E S *

When Spencer W. Kimball was courting his wife, Camilla, he ate with her family quite regularly. He later said, "Father Eyring gave his consent to our marriage just to get rid of me" (Kimball, "Spencer W. Kimball," *BYU Studies* 25[4]: 62).

67

DEATH AND IMMORTALITY

* JOKES *

An elderly sister passed away having never married. On top of her dresser was a paper with complete instructions for her funeral—the songs, the speakers, the prayers. At the bottom, as a special addendum, was the following note: "You must have *no* male pallbearers. Since they wouldn't take me out when I was living, they can't take me out when I'm dead."

* QUOTATIONS *

J. Golden Kimball: I like to preach a man's funeral sermon while he's living. You can't tell the truth about a man when he is dead. I've given many a man a ticket to the celestial glory that I knew wouldn't take him halfway there (Cheney, *Golden Legacy*, 96).

* * *

Garrison Keillor: They say such nice things about people at their funerals that it makes me sad to realize that I'm going to miss mine by just a few days.

* * *

J. Golden Kimball: When it comes to self-sacrifice, fighting for the truth, [some people] are like the dying man who was asked by the minister, "Will you denounce the devil and all his workings?" The dying man looked up in a feeble and distressed way and said, "Please don't ask me to do that. I am going to a strange country, and I don't want to make any enemies" (Conference Report, Oct. 1912, 27).

* STORIES *

President David O. McKay entered the elevator in the Hotel Utah one day to find a boy who shook the president's hand with admiring awe. The young man got off the elevator a floor below Brother McKay's apartment. But when the Prophet, who moved very slowly with the help of a companion, finally exited on his floor, he was surprised to see the same boy standing in the hall panting from his race up the stairway, and with his hand extended for another shake. "I just wanted to shake hands with you once more before you die," the boy explained (Gibbons, *David O. McKay*, 232–33).

* * *

Charles Dillingham and Florenz Ziegfeld, both eminent producers and both now deceased, were pallbearers at the funeral of the great escape artist, Houdini. As they lifted the beautiful and heavy casket to their shoulders, Dillingham whispered to Ziegfeld, "Suppose he isn't here."

* * *

The great American actor W. C. Fields was famous for his raspy voice, his bulbous nose, and the drunken, rascally characters he played. It is said that when he was on his death bed, a friend came to visit him and was astonished to find him reading the Bible. His friend asked, "Bill, what in the world are you doing reading the Bible?"

Fields's reply was, "Looking for loopholes."

* * *

Mark Twain once went to a dinner party where the chief subject of conversation was heaven and hell. Twain sat in silence throughout the conversation. Finally a woman asked, "Why do you not say anything? I would like to hear your opinion."

"Madam, you must excuse me," Twain replied. "I am silent of necessity—I have friends in both places."

* * *

Spencer W. Kimball and Bruce R. McConkie once traveled to Mexico City to visit the mission. The heat was oppressive, so they took off their coats during a break in the meetings. When it was time for the next session, Elder Kimball put on Elder McConkie's coat, which hung down past his hands, and Elder McConkie pulled on the small coat, which came just to his forearms. The missionaries raced for their cameras.

Later, at Oaxaca, a guide showed the two men a large column and explained its folklore: if a man reached his arms around the column, the number of finger widths between his hands would equal the number of years he had remaining. Elder McConkie's long arms actually overlapped by sixteen years. "That," Elder Kimball explained, "means that you are already dead and don't know it" (Kimball, "Spencer W. Kimball," *BYU Studies* 25[4]: 64).

* * *

It seems that two members of a stake, both endowed, were critically ill and neither was expected to live. The person in charge of burial clothes telephoned the stake president one night, exercised over the possibility of two funerals and only one set of burial clothes. "What shall I do?" he asked the president.

The president, seeing no solution, said he would just have to work it out himself, for there would not be time to send to Church headquarters for the clothing. Then he forgot the incident. He was reminded of it when he saw that person at a meeting some weeks later. "How did you come out with your problem?" he inquired.

"All right," said the man, "no trouble."

"What did you do?" the president inquired.

"Oh," he answered, "I went out and administered to one of them" (Packer, *Teach Ye Diligently*, 251–52).

DEBT

* JOKES *

A debtor on the witness stand cried, "As God is my judge, I do not owe the money."

The judge replied, "He is not. I am. You do."

* QUOTATIONS *

J. Golden Kimball: I can tell you how you can keep out of debt; but I can't tell you how to get out after you get in. I had a man come to me the other day who wanted me to endorse his note. I had sworn, almost on an oath, I would never sign another note, not even for my wife. But he looked at me so pitifully, and was in such dire distress, and I had so much confidence in him, that I told him I would sign it, although I was quite sure I could not pay it if he did not. He applied at one of our banks. They did not know me, for which I was very thankful. I went to the bank and looked the man in the face. He said: "Mr. Kimball, haven't you got any collaterals?" I said: "Collaterals—I should say not! I haven't got a collateral of any kind." He said, "How do you expect me to take your endorsement?" I replied, "On my looks and general character. That is all I have got." And he turned me down; and I have been tickled to death ever since. That is the way to keep out of debt (Conference Report, Oct. 1921, 85).

DILIGENCE

* JOKES *

A golfer hit his ball into a deadly sand trap, where it landed in a bed of ants. The golfer stepped up to the ball, swung mightily, and missed, flinging ants all over the adjacent green. The remaining ants scurried around crazily. The golfer drew back his club and swung again, slaughtering a few hundred more ants. One bright ant who had been watching this terrible event scrambled up on the ball and shouted, "Hey, everyone. If we want to be saved we've got to get on the ball!"

* QUOTATIONS *

J. Golden Kimball to a group of less active men: You are like me. You have been ordained to the priesthood of God in this church and there is no such thing as resigning from the priesthood. When you joined the Church and received the priesthood, you made a covenant with God and you can't resign unless you leave the Church or commit a sin and get disfellowshipped. Let's pull together. Suppose I do everything the Lord wants me to do and when I leave this life he says, "Good boy, Golden, go on up there." And I am exalted to the highest place and you people lag behind and fail. What fun can I have up there playing the jew's-harp and talking to myself and knowing you fellows are stuck in the mud somewheres? (Cheney, *Golden Legacy*, 97–98).

DIRECTION

* JOKES *

If you think you're confused, think of Christopher Columbus. First off, he didn't know where he was going. When he got there, he didn't know where he was. And when he got back home, he didn't know where he'd been!

* * *

"Caddy, why do you keep looking at your watch?"
"Pardon me, sir. This is not a watch; it's a compass."

* QUOTATIONS *

Orson Hyde: I like to hear an energetic speaker; but one who speaks very loud is apt to injure himself. When I have spoken too loudly, I have done injustice to myself and probably to the congregation. . . . At the same time, I do not want my mind so trammelled as brother Parley P. Pratt's once was, when dancing was first introduced into Nauvoo among the Saints. I observed brother Parley standing in the figure, and he was making no motion particularly, only up and down. Says I, "Brother Parley, why don't you move forward?" Says he, "When I think which way I am going, I forget the step; and when I think of the step, I forget which way to go" (*Journal of Discourses* 6:150).

* * *

Marvin J. Ashton: Our journey through life must be charted. We must know where we're going.

I'm reminded of a man in New York who jumped into a taxicab

and said, "Hurry, hurry, I'm late!" The cab driver took off with a lurch and wove rapidly through traffic.

Suddenly his passenger said, "Oh, I forgot to tell you where to go."

"I know," said the cabbie, "but we are surely making good time" (*New Era,* July 1981, 17).

* * *

George Durrant: I have been told that a traveler driving through Manti, Utah, stopped, rolled down his car window, and asked a farmer . . . , "How do I get to Salt Lake from here?"

The farmer replied, "You can go up several miles, then turn left and go through Moroni, then continue on to Nephi. Get on the freeway and head north to Salt Lake. Or you can go past the turnoff and go up through Thistle and then down Spanish Fork Canyon to the freeway. Go north and you'll get to Salt Lake."

After considering the alternatives, the visitor asked, "Does it matter which way I go?"

The farmer . . . replied, "Not to me it don't" (Durrant, *Look at the Sky,* 1).

* * *

George Durrant: Two beginning but lucky deer hunters had shot a big buck. They were dragging it to camp when an experienced hunter coming up the trail observed that they were pulling it by its hind legs. He helpfully suggested, "If you fellers would pull the deer by the horns, you'll be dragging it with the grain of the hair, and it will go more easily."

Taking this advice, the hunters took hold of the horns and dragged the deer for another hour. Finally one said to the other, "He was right; it does drag easier this way."

"Yes," replied the other, "but we're getting farther and farther away from camp" (Durrant, *Look at the Sky,* 2).

*   S T O R I E S   *

During his 1846 campaign for Congress, Abraham Lincoln attended a sermon by evangelist Peter Cartwright, who called for all who wanted to go to heaven to stand. Everyone rose but Lincoln. Then the preacher gave a call for all who wanted to avoid hell. Again everyone stood but Lincoln.

"I am grieved," said the preacher, "to see Abe Lincoln sitting back there unmoved by these appeals. If he doesn't want to go to heaven and doesn't want to escape hell, will he tell us where he does want to go?"

At that, Lincoln stood. "I'm going to Congress," he said.

* * *

Because David [O. McKay] and [his wife Emma] Ray lived the ideals of the Church in their home, spiritual things came naturally to their children. Typical of this is the experience of one of the sons when he was a small boy. One day he was visiting his grandfather's home, which was next door, while spring house cleaning and re-papering of the rooms were in progress. The little fellow . . . stood in a doorway watching the work and attracted the attention of a workman [who] asked him, "When you are a man, would you like to be a painter and paper-hanger?" Without hesitation the child answered, "No, sir." The workman persisted, and said, "Then what would you like to be?" The boy . . . replied seriously, "I should like to be a 'Twelve Apostle'" (Morrell, *Highlights in the Life of President David O. McKay,* 42).

* * *

DISCIPLINE

* JOKES *

At a parent-teacher conference, a mother told the teacher, "My son Paul is a very sensitive boy."

"Yes," said the teacher, "I've noticed that. Is there anything we should do about it?"

"Well," said the mother, "if Paul misbehaves, please spank the boy next to him."

* STORIES *

Joseph Fielding Smith: It wasn't much of a whipping. . . . [My father] did it because he thought I had lied to him. He didn't do it because I had done something wrong, but because he thought I hadn't told him the truth. And so he gave me a cut or two across the back. Years afterwards I said to him one day, "Do you remember when you gave me a lashing?" and told him the circumstances, "because you thought I had told you an untruth?"

"Now," he said," "I don't know that I remember a thing like that."

"Well," I said, "it happened. . . ."

"Oh, well," he said, "we'll let that apply on something you did when you didn't get caught" (Joseph Fielding McConkie, *True and Faithful,* 19–20).

DISCOVERY

* QUOTATIONS *

Orson F. Whitney: Columbus was one of a number of learned men who held that the earth was a sphere. While not the first to hold that theory, he was [among] the first to put it into practice. He believed that he could reach India by sailing westward. Accordingly, he sailed for India, and found America on the way. [President Joseph F. Smith, under his breath, from his seat behind the speaker: "He could hardly have missed it."] (see Conference Report, Oct. 1918, 39).

EFFICIENCY

* STORIES *

According to a story of uncertain origin, an efficiency expert was hired to make a report on the New York Philharmonic Orchestra. As a part of this preparation, he attended several concerts. At last, he issued his report, which read in part as follows:

"For considerable periods, the four oboe players have nothing to do. Their number should be reduced and the work spread more evenly over the whole of the concert, thus eliminating peaks of activity. . . . All twelve first violins were playing identical notes. This seems unnecessary duplication. . . . Much effort was absorbed in the playing of semiquavers. This seems an excessive refinement. It is recommended that all notes be rounded up to the nearest quaver. . . . No useful purpose is served by the repeating on the horns a passage which has already been played by the strings. . . . It is estimated that if all redundant passages were eliminated, the whole concert time of two hours could be reduced to twenty minutes and there would be no need for an intermission."

Enemies

* QUOTATIONS *

Toast given by Elder Jedediah M. Grant at an 1849 Pioneer Day celebration: "To Martin Van Buren and all mobocrats: May they be winked at by blind men, kicked across lots by cripples, nibbled to death by ducks, and carried to hell through the keyhole by bumblebees" (quoted in Parry and Morris, *Mormon Book of Lists*, 29).

* * *

A toast between the devil and Joseph Smith, as written by Parley P. Pratt:

Devil: Here's to my good friend, Joe Smith, may all sorts of ill-luck befall him, and may he never be suffered to enter my kingdom, either in time or eternity, for he would almost make me forget that I am a devil, and make a gentleman of me, while he gently overthrows my government at the same time that he wins my friendship.

Smith: Here to his Satanic Majesty: may he be driven from the earth and be forced to put to sea in a stone canoe with an iron paddle, and may the canoe sink, and a shark swallow the canoe and its royal freight and an alligator swallow the shark and may the alligator be bound in the northwest corner of hell, and the door be locked, key lost, and a blind man hunting for it (Cracroft and Lambert, *A Believing People*, 265).

ENTHUSIASM

* QUOTATIONS *

J. Golden Kimball: A [man] had a mule which balked, and he could not get it to move; so he went into a drug store and asked the druggist if he had anything that he thought would start the mule. The druggist came out and injected something in the region of the ribs of the mule, and immediately thereafter the [man] saw a streak of dust and the animal flying over the hill. He went back to the druggist and said, "How much is it?" "Twenty-five cents." "Well," said he, "Just put fifty cents worth in me, so I can catch the mule" (Conference Report, Apr. 1906, 19–20).

* STORIES *

A short time before his death, Elder LeGrand Richards was asked by a stake president, "Brother Richards, how are you feeling?"

The ninety-five-year-old apostle said, "Well, President. My body, the house I live in, is getting old and creaky. But the real LeGrand Richards is still on fire!" (*A Time to Laugh*, 9).

* * *

Rev. Samuel J. May: "Mr. Garrison, you are too excited—you are on fire!"

William Lloyd Garrison: "I have need to be on fire, for I have icebergs around me to melt."

EXAMPLE

* Q U O T A T I O N S *

Spencer W. Kimball: Long years ago when I was in the presidency of the St. Joseph Stake in Arizona, one Sabbath day I filled an assignment in the Eden Ward. . . .

As the meeting proceeded, my eye was attracted to seven little boys on the front seat of the chapel. I was delighted that they were in this ward conference. I made a mental note, then shifted my interest to other things. Soon my attention was focused on the seven little boys again.

It seemed strange to me that each of the seven raised his right leg and put it over the left knee, and then in a moment all would change at the same time and put the left leg over the right knee. I thought it was unusual, but I just ignored it.

In a moment or two, all in unison brushed their hair with their right hands; then all seven boys leaned lightly on their wrists and supported their faces by their hands, and then simultaneously they went back to the crossing of their legs again.

It all seemed so strange, and I wondered about it as I was trying to think of what I was going to say in the meeting. And then suddenly it came to me like a bolt of lightning: These boys were mimicking me!

That day I learned the lesson of my life—that we who are in positions of authority must be careful indeed, because others watch us and find in us their examples (*Ensign*, Nov. 1974, 79).

* * *

N. Eldon Tanner: The Singing Mothers this afternoon, pardon me, the singing for this afternoon session will be furnished by the Brigham Young University. I hope you do as well as your mothers (Conference Report, Oct. 1964, 61).

* S T O R I E S *

In 1928 N. Eldon Tanner, then thirty years old, was called as second counselor in the bishopric of his Cardston, Alberta, ward. He was directly responsible for the deacons and also served as Scout leader. He soon noted that not many of the young men were attending priesthood meeting. Visiting with some of the deacons, he learned that many of them had only overalls or coveralls to wear, and few had Sunday clothes. For Brother Tanner, "principle was absolute but fashion was negotiable." He therefore went to each deacon and offered a deal. If they would come to priesthood meeting, he too would wear coveralls. The result was one hundred percent activity among the three deacons quorums of his ward (Durham, *N. Eldon Tanner*, 43–44).

EXCELLENCE

* Q U O T A T I O N S *

Kenneth Boulding, professor of economics at the University of Colorado: If you pursue excellence, happiness sneaks up behind you and touches you on the shoulder. If you pursue mediocrity, you're sure to catch it.

Excuses

* J O K E S *

"Tell the court how you came to take the car."
"Your honor, the car was standing in front of the cemetery, and I thought the owner was dead."

* * *

A driver tucked this note under the windshield wiper of his automobile: "I've circled the block for twenty minutes. I'm late for an appointment and if I don't park here I'll lose my job. 'Forgive us our trespasses.'"

When he came back he found a parking ticket and this note: "I've circled the block for twenty years and if I don't give you a ticket, I'll lose my job. 'Lead us not into temptation.'"

Expectations

* Q U O T A T I O N S *

The "ninth beatitude," invented by Alexander Pope: "Blessed is he who expects nothing, for he shall never be disappointed."

EXPERIENCE

* J O K E S *

If we could all sell our experiences for what they have cost us, we'd be rich.

* Q U O T A T I O N S *

Brigham Young: I was reminded of the anecdote of the [boy's] attempt at shooting a squirrel. His [father] having occasion to be absent from home, charged him to be sure and not meddle with his guns and ammunition; but no sooner had the [father] got fairly out of the way, when the [boy's] curiosity prompted him to try one of the . . . guns; he accordingly took one down which had been loaded for some time, and went into the woods. He soon saw a squirrel, and crept up a hill behind a log and fired, but the gun being heavily charged, it knocked the [boy] over, and he rolled down the hill.

Upon gaining his equilibrium and realizing his defeat, he looked up from the ground where he lay, and seeing the squirrel jumping from tree to tree as if conscious of victory, he cried,—"Well, well, cuffy, if you had been at the other end of the gun you would have known more about it" (Brigham Young History, 1801–44, 144–45).

FAITH

* JOKES *

In a rural, quite religious farm community, there was a disastrous drought and the crops were dying. In desperation, the local preacher announced that the whole community would assemble at the edge of one of the fields and pray for rain. A large crowd gathered, and the preacher climbed on a bale of hay and surveyed the flock. He said, "Brothers and sisters, you have come here to pray for rain."

"Amen!" responded the crowd.

"Well," said the preacher, "do you have sufficient faith?"

"Amen! Amen!" shouted the crowd.

"All right, all right," said the preacher, "but I have one question to ask you."

The crowd stood silent, puzzled, expectant.

"Brothers and sisters," said the preacher, "where are your umbrellas?"

* * *

A man was mountain climbing when he stumbled and fell over the edge of a cliff. He grabbed onto a thin tree branch and hung there in midair. He'd never been a praying man, but now, frightened, he looked up to heaven and called, "Is anybody up there?"

A peaceful voice came to him. "Yes, my son. Let go of the branch, and I will save you."

The man paused a moment, then asked, "Uh . . . is anyone *else* up there?"

* * *

A very religious man lived in a house by a great river. One night there was a terrible flood and the man had to climb up on the roof of his house to escape being drowned.

After a time some men came by in a boat to rescue him, but he refused. "I have faith that God will rescue me." Soon after, another boat came to rescue him, and again he refused: "I have faith in God."

Considerably later a helicopter flew over and let down a rope ladder, but the man waved them away, shouting, "I have faith in God to rescue me!"

At last, the force of the water broke up the house and the man was drowned. He went to heaven, and when he saw God he said, "I had such faith in you, and you let me drown. Why?"

"What do you mean, let you drown? I sent you two boats and a helicopter."

* * *

A young girl's father had been in the hospital for a serious operation, and for several days he could not receive visitors. Still in pretty bad shape, he was finally allowed a visit from his family. His young daughter was baffled by her father's condition. "But, Dad, you look awful! Didn't you get my get-well card?"

* * *

A gala crowd gathered for the test run of Robert Fulton's outlandish steamboat contraption *The Clermont*. For hours the strange craft belched smoke and sparks from its tall, thin stack as his engineers attempted to get up the necessary head of steam. When the time to cast off had come and the engines were being limbered up, the boat vibrated violently and made a loud racket. A group of doubting Thomases in the crowd had been shouting loudly and scornfully, "She'll never start! She'll never start!" But the boat pulled itself together and started to move up the river. After a moment of astonished silence, the voices of the scoffers resumed their shouts, this time crying with all the scorn they could muster, "She'll never stop! She'll never stop!"

* * *

An old woman on a sinking ship was told they had no other hope but to trust in Providence.

"Oh dear," she said. "Has it come to that?"

* QUOTATIONS *

George Albert Smith: I went on my Mission to Washington in full faith to ask for the admission of Deseret [as part of the United States], never asking myself the question whether I would accomplish it or not, striving to believe with all the power and faith I could command, that we could accomplish our Mission.

I sometimes sat in the gallery of the House of Representatives and heard the members wrangle, and asked myself if it was possible that the Lord wished us to join hands with such unhallowed confusion and political chicanery. After my return home, some of the brethren asked me how much faith I had that we should be admitted. I concluded my faith had been like that of a certain pious lady, whose minister called upon her and inquired concerning her religious welfare. She replied that she was well satisfied with her spiritual progression, but in her temporal welfare she was not equally prosperous. She was destitute of bread and had nothing to sustain life. The minister kindly told her to exercise faith and she could make stones into bread. She thanked him for his timely advice, she had never thought of that, and accordingly went and procured some stones of suitable size for loaves of bread, washed them, put them in pans, heated her oven in which she placed them, closed the door, exclaimed "I have firm faith, that when these stones come out of the oven they will be good bread." After patiently waiting the proper time, she opened the oven door and looked anxiously in; "there!" she declared, "they are stones yet, and I knew they would be all the time" (*Journal of Discourses* 9:263–64).

*   S T O R I E S   *

Elder Matthew Cowley went to visit eight-year-old Joe, lying unconscious in a hospital, and gave him a blessing. The boy was breathing with the aid of an iron lung after having contracted polio and pneumonia.

A short while later he visited little Joe again, and lying in an adjoining bed was another young fellow. Elder Cowley visited with Joe for a few moments, and as he was about to leave, Joe asked Elder Cowley to give his roommate a blessing too.

Two weeks after that, Elder Cowley visited young Joe a third time in the hospital, and this time Joe was rather sad.

"I am lonely," he said. "Maybe I shouldn't have asked you to bless my partner. He got well so soon and has gone home" (*Matthew Cowley Speaks,* 69).

* * *

A Church member who was lying in the hospital waiting for surgery was visited by Elder J. Golden Kimball. This is the record written of the visit: "The day before the dreadful ordeal, a mutual friend brought Brother J. Golden Kimball to administer to me. First, he talked and visited a considerable time and then blessed me. There was nothing frivolous about his talk, and yet he soon had me smiling. Later, the smiles were interspersed with laughter. I began to see things in proper perspective and to realize that all was well with the world and that the sky for me, after all, had but one dark cloud in it which, probably, would soon roll away. I felt I was in the presence of a sane, well balanced man and a man of exceptionally strong faith. In truth, never did I feel the power of faith more than that day" (Richards, *J. Golden Kimball,* 102).

FAMILY

* JOKES *

Teenage son: Mom, I really love you. I appreciate all that you do for me.

Mother: Why, thank you, Nate. It's nice to hear a young man express such tender feelings.

Teenage daughter: So, Nate—your teachers quorum adviser gave out an assignment, huh?

* * *

Father: Son, when I was your age, my family was so poor that all I had to wear was hand-me-down clothes!

Son: That's not so bad, Dad. I wear hand-me-downs sometimes.

Father: Yes, but all I had was older sisters!

* * *

Emily was an only child and badly wanted a sister or brother. She prayed night after night that God would send one to her home. Nothing changed, so at length she gave up praying for that particular blessing. After quite some time, her mother learned she was expecting. She went to the hospital and gave birth to not one baby but twins.

When she heard the news, Emily exclaimed, "Well, it's a good thing I stopped praying when I did!"

* QUOTATIONS *

Heber J. Grant: The first great commandment is to "multiply and replenish the earth;" and Utah's best crop is babies (Conference Report, Apr. 1921, 211).

* * *

John M. Knight: My grandfathers and great grandfathers and grandmothers, and my father and mother passed through all the trials incident to the pioneering of this great western wilderness, and they were faithful to the truth. I ask for no greater legacy than that, because their lives were an inspiration to me, and they encouraged me in living the principles of the gospel. I mentioned this fact in Denver, that I represented the fourth generation in the Church, and our baby, a little fellow of seven years, went to his mother and said: "What do you think father called us in meeting?" And she said: "I don't know, son, what was it?" He said: "Father said that we were the fifth amendment" (Conference Report, Oct. 1922, 42).

* * *

Elaine Cannon: You've no doubt heard about the young girl who complained to her teenage brother about the terrible blows that life had dealt her. And she said, "It just isn't fair; you got the curly hair and the straight nose."

And he said, "Well, you got the curly nose and the straight hair!" (*Ensign*, May 1982, 95).

* * *

Ogden Nash: A family is a unit composed not only of children, but of men, women, an occasional animal, and the common cold.

* * *

Will Rogers: Live that you wouldn't be ashamed to sell the family parrot to the town gossip.

* STORIES *

Once when Abraham Lincoln was carrying two of his sons, Willie and Tad, and both were yelling at the top of their lungs, he was asked what was wrong.

"Just what's the matter with the whole world. I've got three walnuts and each wants two."

FATHERHOOD

* JOKES *

A well-adjusted father is the man who can drive along and enjoy the scenery—even with kids in the back seat.

* * *

A father is a man who has snapshots in his wallet where his money used to be.

* * *

A bishop's wife took her overworked husband to the family doctor. After examining him, the doctor took the wife aside and whispered: "I don't like the way your husband looks."

"I don't either," she replied, "but he's always been a good father to the children."

FEAR

* QUOTATIONS *

J. Golden Kimball: I attended a Round-Up on the Fair Grounds and almost lost my life when that grand-stand with three or four thousand people on it burned down, in ten minutes. My brother Elias and I happened to be on the topmost seat, because it was the cheapest. We were about the last to get out. I said: "Elias, the Lord is with us again. Praised be the name of the Lord." I tried not to be frightened, but you ought to have seen inside of me before I got off that stand (Conference Report, Oct. 1924, 72).

* * *

J. Golden Kimball: I spent five years in the Southern States, and filled my first mission, in 1883, when they killed elders. I was with Elder Roberts, and I know all about that experience. I never got much notoriety out of it, but I know something about it, just as much as anyone who was there, I know what it means to smell powder, and I am glad of it, and I thank the Lord I did not run. I guess I would have done so, but I had no place to go (Conference Report, Oct. 1917, 133).

FORGIVENESS

* STORIES *

When Frederick the Great was seized with his mortal illness, he asked an advisor whether it was necessary to forgive all his enemies. On receiving the proper answer, he said to the queen, "Dorothy, write to your brother that I forgive him all the evil he has done me; but wait till I am dead first."

FRIENDSHIP

* STORIES *

As a General Authority, Spencer W. Kimball traveled a lot, and he loved to joke with his friends. He wrote to one, "I thought you might have been at the depot as my train went through at five this morning." To another he wrote, "I looked down as my airplane passed over your town today but didn't see you out and around" (Kimball, "Spencer W. Kimball," *BYU Studies* 25[4]: 67).

GENEALOGY

* J O K E S *

A wealthy family hired a professional genealogist to trace their lineage. After a few months, the genealogist discovered that one ancestor had been hanged for stealing horses. Not wanting to embarrass the family, the genealogist reported, "John died suddenly 8 June 1812 when the platform on which he was standing, gave way. . . ."

GOALS

* J O K E S *

At basic training a sergeant was training a bunch of recruits at the rifle range. He had the men line up at a hundred yards and told them to fire. They did so—but when the smoke cleared the sergeant saw the target was untouched. He had them move forward fifty yards and try again. The results were the same. He had them try it at twenty-five yards. Not one mark on the target.

Finally, exasperated, the sergeant faced his troops and yelled, "Fix bayonets and charge!"

GOD

J. Golden Kimball: I may not have a perfect and true conception of God, but I love God; I love him for his perfection; I love him for his mercy; I love him for his justice; and notwithstanding my many weaknesses I am not afraid to meet him. For I know that he will deal justly by me; and the great joy I will have is that he will understand me and that is more than some of you have been able to do (Conference Report, Oct. 1919, 205).

* * *

Orson F. Whitney: One of our "Mormon" boys out on a mission was confronted with this question. He had just been preaching that the Father and the Son appeared to Joseph Smith, when a voice rang out: "No man hath seen God at any time." The boy had his wits about him. "Of course not," said he, "God is a business man—you can't see him at any time; you have to make a special appointment with him" (Conference Report, Oct. 1924, 22).

When Mark Twain was getting on in years a lady came to visit him. "I just love your work," she said, leaning down to kiss his hand. "How God must love you!"

"I hope so," the author responded. But when she was gone he turned to a companion and said, "I guess she hasn't heard of our strained relations."

GOSSIP

* JOKES *

Shelly: So is that it? Is that the whole story?
Katherine: I should hope so! I've already told you quite a bit more than I heard!

* * *

The ward gossip could hardly wait to rush up to the group of Relief Society sisters. She lowered her voice and said, "You all know I don't like to repeat gossip—so I'm only going to say this once!"

GOVERNMENT

* JOKES *

A little boy who had lost his father noticed that his widowed mother was having a hard time making ends meet. He wrote a letter to the Lord and said, "Dear Heavenly Father, please send Mom a hundred dollars to help with the family."

The letter ended up on the postmaster general's desk, and he was quite touched by it. So he took a twenty-dollar bill from his wallet and put it in an official postmaster general envelope and sent it to the little boy.

About two weeks later he got a letter back that said, "Dear God, thank you for all that you have done. But we need another hundred dollars. And if you don't mind, when you send it to Mom, please

95

don't route it through the U.S. mail, because last time the government deducted 80 percent of it!"

GRATITUDE

* JOKES *

Many years ago, an Idaho farmer bought a horse from his bishop. "Now, this is no ordinary horse," said the bishop, a very religious man. "He doesn't respond to 'Giddyap.' When you want him to get moving, you've got to say 'Thank heaven!' And when you want him to stop, don't say 'Whoa.' Say 'Amen' instead."

The farmer thanked the bishop, paid him for the horse, and went on his way, with a cheerful "Thank heaven!" to get the horse going. Pretty soon the farmer noticed that the wooden bridge ahead had washed away, leaving a hazardous dropoff to the river fifty feet below. In a panic, the farmer tried to remember his instructions. After saying, "Whoa!" and "Stop!" and "Halt!" he finally remembered and called out, "Amen!" The horse stopped short right on the edge of the steep riverbank. That's when the farmer, relieved that he had averted disaster, called out, "Thank heaven!"

* * *

There's something kind of sad about atheists: when they feel grateful for their blessings, they have no one to thank.

* * *

In some parts of Mexico hot springs and cold springs are found side by side. The women often boil their clothes in the hot springs and rinse them in the cold springs. A tourist, who had been watching this procedure, remarked to his Mexican friend, "I guess they think old Mother Nature is pretty generous."

"No, señor," the other replied. "There is much grumbling because she supplies no soap."

* * *

A merchant was carrying some goods to market in his wagon. On the way he met a beggar trudging along with a heavy pack on his shoulders. The merchant felt sorry for him and asked him to get into the wagon.

As they rode on in silence the merchant saw that the beggar was sitting with his pack still on his shoulders.

"Why don't you put your pack down?" he asked in surprise.

"Bless you," said the man, "it's enough that you're carrying me! Do I have to burden you with my pack besides?"

* * *

Aunt Lois: Johnny, I'm shocked that you don't appreciate my birthday gift to you. After all, I did ask whether you wanted a big check or a small one.

Johnny (sheepishly): Sorry, Aunt Lois. I just didn't realize you meant neckties!

* * *

A mother gave her son two neckties for his birthday, and the next Sunday when he dressed for church, he wore one of the ties. His mom noticed it and instantly got all cross and huffy. "What, you don't like the other tie?" she asked.

* STORIES *

It was said that Oliver Cromwell, the English statesman and soldier, usually said the following blessing before meals: "Some people have food but no appetite; others have appetite, but no food. I have both. The Lord be praised."

* * *

A rancher in Kamas, at the base of Utah's Uinta mountains, decided he wanted to sell his ranch. He hired a real estate agent, who came out to inspect his property and write up an ad.

Later the realtor called the rancher to go over the ad copy with him before placing it in the paper. "For sale," read the realtor, "Picturesque white frame ranch house with white picket fence and eighty acres of rich farmland in the middle of beautiful Kamas Valley. Clear streams of mountain water flow nearby, well stocked with rainbow trout. House faces rugged mountain peaks and is located in a small, friendly farming community with good schools and a new church."

"Stop!" said the rancher. "The deal's off! This is the kind of place I've wanted all my life!" (Nash, *Lengthen Your Smile*, 205).

* * *

Mom was helping two-year-old Henry with his prayers one night. She would say a line, then have him repeat it. The prayer was going well until Mom said, "I thank thee for all thy blessings." Henry responded graciously, "You're welcome."

HAPPINESS

The U.S. Declaration of Independence guarantees citizens "life, liberty, and the pursuit of happiness." Benjamin Franklin, who helped draft the great document, pointed out later that the document doesn't guarantee happiness but only its pursuit. "You have to catch up with it yourself," he said.

HEAVEN

"Who wants to go to heaven?" the Sunday School teacher asked. All the children but one raised their hands.

"Billy, don't you want to go to heaven when you die?"

"Oh, sure. I thought you were getting together a group to go now."

* * *

A teacher smiled pleasantly at her Primary class. "All right, children, all those who want to go to heaven raise your hands."

Everyone responded but one little boy. "What's the matter, Shawn? Don't you want to go to heaven?" asked the teacher.

"I can't, Sister Nelson. My mom said I had to come straight home."

* S T O R I E S *

An acquaintance met J. Golden Kimball on the street one day and in conversation asked, "Do you believe that Jonah was swallowed by the whale?"

"When I get to heaven I'll ask Jonah," J. Golden answered.

"But," said the man, "what if Jonah is not there?"

"Then you will have to ask him" (Cheney, *Golden Legacy,* 109).

HOME TEACHING

* J O K E S *

Two home teachers went out one night to visit their families. At one home, they could hear activity inside, but no one would answer the door, even though they knocked repeatedly. Finally, the senior companion took out a piece of paper and wrote, "Revelation 3:20: 'Behold, I stand at the door and knock: If any man hear my voice, and open the door, I will come in to him.'" Then he put the paper under the door.

The next Sunday, the member returned the piece of paper to the home teacher. Below the home teacher's message was written "Genesis 3:10: 'I was afraid, because I was naked; and I hid myself.'"

HONESTY

* J O K E S *

The Gospel Doctrine teacher said, "Next Sunday, for our lesson on honesty, I'd like you to read the 17th chapter of Mark." On the following Sunday, the teacher stood up and said, "Now then, all of you who have done as I requested and read the 17th chapter of Mark, please raise your hands." Nearly every hand in the congregation went up. Then said the teacher, "You are the very people I want to talk to. There is no 17th chapter of Mark!"

* * *

Teacher: Rachel, I hope I didn't see you looking at Johnny's paper during the test.

Rachel: I hope not, too.

* * *

The train came to a sudden stop. People started to look out of the window and then hurriedly dropped back into their seats as they saw that the cause of the stop was a hold-up.

The robbers came through the train ruthlessly stripping the money, jewels, and valuables from the passengers.

One man seemed to become more and more nervous as the bandits approached the seat where he sat with his friend. Finally, drawing a ten-dollar bill from his pocket he leaned toward his friend and said, "Here, Jerry. Here's the ten dollars I owe you."

* * *

Father (looking at son's report card): Well, son, there's one good thing about these marks. With grades like this, you couldn't possibly have cheated in school.

* * *

As the caravan slowly moved through the burning desert, two camels plodded along together. Finally one of them looked around, made sure no one was within earshot, and muttered to his fellow camel, "I don't care *what* everybody says. I'm thirsty!"

* * *

The owner of an old-fashioned grocery store in a small country town was fond of quoting a scripture after each sale. His ability to produce a scripture for all occasions never ceased to amuse the old-timers who hung around the store, and they would listen closely to see what verse he would come up with next.

A woman purchased some fabric and he said, "Proverbs 31:13—She seeketh wool, and flax, and worketh willingly with her hands."

As a man bought a sack of flour, he said "Matthew 4:4—Man shall not live by bread alone."

A little boy bought some candy and as he rung up the sale he quoted, "Mark 10:14—Suffer the little children to come unto me."

It was nearly closing time when the little bells above the door jangled loudly. A well-dressed young man, obviously a stranger from out of town, entered.

"Help you?" offered the proprietor.

"I need a blanket for my horse," said the man. "He's out in his trailer and it's too cold for just one. Bring me the nicest blanket you've got!"

The store owner went into the back room and returned with a brown blanket. "That'll be five dollars."

"Five dollars? You've got to be kidding!' said the man. "This horse is a thoroughbred. He gets only the best! He wouldn't stand still for an old five-dollar blanket."

Without comment, the store owner took back the blanket, then merely selected another of a different color and brought it out. "This one's twenty-five dollars."

"Now, look," said the young man. "Perhaps I didn't make myself plain. This isn't just any old horse! He's worth thousands! Now I want the best, most expensive blanket you've got! Comprende?"

The owner once more went into the store room, pulled out another color of the same material and quality, and brought it back. "This is the only one left, and it's one hundred dollars."

"Now that's more like it!" the fellow said enthusiastically as he paid. Throwing the five-dollar blanket over his shoulder, he left.

The old-timers stared silently at the shopkeeper as they waited to see what possible scripture he could come up with for that sale! Going behind the register, he rang up the hundred dollars and said, "Matthew 25:38—He was a stranger, and I took him in."

* * *

A bishop decided to visit one of the families in his ward. On the appointed afternoon, he was formally greeted and shown into family's spotless living room. The bishop looked around, smiled at the family, and said, "I'm glad to see you are living so comfortably."

A young daughter spoke up. "Oh, Bishop, if you want to know how we really live, you must come when you're not here."

* * *

Mrs. Grannum accused her neighbor Mrs. Johnson:

"Mrs. Johnson, when you returned my eggbeater, I found you had broken it. What are you going to do about it?"

Mrs. Johnson replied: "That's ridiculous. In the first place, I never borrowed your eggbeater. Furthermore, it was in good condition when I brought it back. And, anyway, it was broken when you lent it to me."

* * *

The bishop approached a young man in the ward. "I understand you went to the ball game instead of coming to church this morning."

"That's a lie," said the boy. "And here's the fish to prove it."

* * *

Have you ever noticed that the very best highway safety device is your rear-view mirror—with a police car in it?

* * *

A woman lost her handbag in the shopping mall and was delighted when an honest young boy returned it to her several hours later. As she looked through her wallet, she did notice one odd thing. "Strange," she said. "When I lost the purse, there was a ten-dollar bill in it. Now I notice there are ten one-dollar bills."

"That's true, ma'am," said the boy. "The last time I found a person's wallet, he didn't have any change to give me for a reward."

* * *

Mom: Son, are you lying again?
Son: I don't tell lies, Mom. I just remember big.

* * *

Stranger: Catch any fish?
Fisherman: Did I! I took thirty out of this stream this morning.
Stranger: Do you know who I am? I'm the game warden.
Fisherman: Do you know who I am? I'm the biggest liar in the country.

* * *

First fisherman: I caught a 250-pound marlin the other day!
Second fisherman: Yeah? Well, I was fishing and hooked a lamp from an old Spanish ship. In fact, the lamp was still lit!
First fisherman: If you'll blow out the light, I'll take 200 pounds off the marlin!

* * *

Mr. Jones and Mr. Brown were having lunch together at the local diner. Repeatedly friends would stop and greet them, and Mr. Jones would tell them in great detail about his recent fishing trip.

Brown listened in amusement, then finally said, "James, I notice that you change the fish's size every time you tell that story."

"Oh, of course," Jones answered. "I never tell a man more than I think he will believe."

* * *

A man tried to sell his neighbor a new dog.

"This is a talking dog," he said. "And you can have him for five dollars."

The neighbor said, "Who do you think you're kidding with this talking dog stuff? There ain't no such animal."

Suddenly the dog looked up with tears in his eyes. "Please buy me, sir," he pleaded. "This man is cruel. He never buys me a meal, never bathes me, never takes me for a walk. And I used to be the richest trick dog in America. I performed before kings. I was in the army and was decorated ten times."

"Hey!" said the neighbor. "He can talk. Why do you want to sell him for just five dollars?"

"Because," said the seller, "I'm getting tired of all his lies."

* * *

In an invitation to the ward to attend tithing settlement, the bishop said, "And now, Brothers and Sisters, let us all give in accordance with what we reported on Form 1040."

* * *

One night a father called on his five-year-old son, Tommy, to say the blessing on the food. The family closed their eyes and bowed their heads and waited . . . and waited . . . and waited. Finally the father got a little anxious. "Tommy," he prompted. "Go ahead."

"But, Dad," said Tommy, his eyes brimming with tears. "If I thank Heavenly Father for the spinach, won't he know I'm telling a lie?"

* QUOTATIONS *

J. Golden Kimball: What can God do for a man who is not honest? You may baptize him every fifteen minutes, but if he does not repent, he will come up out of the water just as dishonest as ever. What can God do for a liar who refuses to repent? Can the Lord save him? He can't claim salvation. Baptising him in water will not settle the trouble, unless you keep him under (Conference Report, Apr. 1909, 37).

* * *

Rulon S. Wells: We have been reading in the papers recently of people called shoplifters, who enter into stores and, when no one is looking, will put an article under their cloak or secret it in some manner and carry it off. One "lady" that I heard of took a beautiful and valuable hat, worth about $30 from a certain dry goods establishment, without being seen. The hat was missed the same night, and all the clerks were asked if they had sold it, but they said they had not. The following Sunday one of the employees of the store discovered a lady at church with this identical hat upon her head. Next Monday morning it was reported, and a bill for $30 was sent to the lady, and a check came back very promptly indeed. I might mention the fact to the ladies that there are some advantages in taking your hats off in church (Conference Report, Oct. 1903, 30).

* * *

Sterling W. Sill: As our family was driving from Arizona, we stopped at a service station, and while the car was being serviced, one of the children said, "Could we have some soda pop?" So we went over to the vending machine. I put in one dime and got out one bottle. I put in another dime and got out another bottle. I put in a third dime, and I got a third bottle. But then the gadget did not lock, and I got the fourth bottle out free. In all, we got four bottles for thirty cents. As I was going over to the car to make the delivery, I thought, *They charge too much for this stuff anyway.* However, I have a little mental night watchman on duty up there in my brain someplace who started to make a fuss. He said, "Look, Sterling, if you're going to be a crook, you had better get more than ten cents out of it."

I don't know just what I would have done if soda water had cost a quarter. But I went back and put the other dime into the machine. Now, how can anyone tell whether I believe in honesty? By what I say about it, or by what I do while I'm over at the vending machine where no one can see me except myself? (*New Era,* Feb. 1973, 44).

* * *

Marvin O. Ashton: I heard this story the other day. It did me good. An antique worshipper . . . was going about in Virginia. He came to a farm where they were doing some advertising of antiques. His eye spied an old man out in the yard chopping wood. In his scrutinizing this thing and that, he went up to the man and the conversation was about as follows: "How do you do?" He said: "It looks like an old axe that you are using." The old man stopped. Said he: "Yes, they have said that this is an axe that George Washington used to use." Of course, the eyes of the antique lover bulged. Exclaimed he, "My dear man, if that is the axe George Washington used, I would give you a right good price for it." The old man grinned. "The only trouble is, if this was the axe that George Washington used, I know this is the third head it has had and the fifth handle" (Conference Report, Apr. 1941, 59).

* * *

Robert Gardner, Jr., a Latter-day Saint who crossed the plains after leaving Nauvoo, told this story about getting ready for the journey: "I went up in Iowa, trying to trade my horses for oxen. I found that oxen had been bought up and were hard to find. I had one horse that was very bad with the heaves. . . .

"I came across a man one day whom I asked if he had any oxen to trade me for that horse. He said no, but he had a fine mare he would give me for him. I went to see her but rode my horse very slow lest he would begin to heave. His mare was a very fine one, but I had to give him fourteen dollars to boot. But I did not want to stay long lest my horse would begin to heave, so I got on the mare and thought I had done it.

"I rode about two miles and passed another man. He asked me if I had bought that mare. I said 'Yes, isn't she a fine one?' He said, 'Yes, but she is stone blind'" (see Madsen, *Journey to Zion*, 267).

* STORIES *

After the prayer book of his wife, Deborah, had been stolen, Benjamin Franklin put the following notice in the *Pennsylvania Gazette:* "Taken out of a pew in the church some months since, a Common Prayer Book, bound in red, gilt, and letters D.F. on each cover. The person who took it is advised to open it and read the Eighth Commandment, and afterwards return it into the same pew again; upon which no further notice will be taken."

* * *

As Marion G. Romney completed law school and passed the bar examination and had begun his law practice, he began to worry about whether or not he could live the standards of the gospel and practice law at the same time. His father was also worried, which added to his concern. It made him wonder if his father had heard the story of a man who walked through a cemetery and stopped to read a headstone that said, "Here lies John Brown, a lawyer and an honest man."

Whereupon the man commented, "I wonder why they buried all three of them in the same grave" (see *New Era,* May 1975, 5).

* * *

A student . . . apparently had been cheating. The teacher called the father in, and the father said, "I don't believe my son, Adam, would cheat."

The teacher said, "We have proof."

"What is your proof?"

"The first question was, Who was the sixteenth president of the United States? The fellow across the aisle from your son wrote Abraham Lincoln and your son, Adam, wrote Abraham Lincoln."

The father said, "Well, they could both be right."

"Yes, but the second question was the tip-off: Who was the seventeenth president of the United States? The fellow across the aisle wrote Lyndon B. Johnson and your son wrote Lyndon B. Johnson."

The father said, "Well, they could both be wrong."

The teacher said, "Well, the third question was the clincher: What were the causes of the Civil War? The fellow across the aisle wrote 'I don't know,' and your son wrote 'Neither do I'" (Featherstone, *Commitment,* 41).

HOPE

* S T O R I E S *

The writer Honoré de Balzac lived many years in a cold and all but empty attic. There was no flame in his fireplace, no picture on his wall. But on one wall he inscribed with charcoal, "Rosewood paneling with commode"; on another, "Gobelin tapestry with Venetian mirror"; and in the place of honor over the fireless grate, "Painting by Raphael."

HOSPITALITY

* STORIES *

Alice James, wife of William James, said that often during evenings her husband would exclaim, "Are we never to have an evening alone? Must we always talk to people every night?" And she would answer, "I will see that whoever calls tonight is told that you are strictly engaged." So they would settle down to their quiet evening. Presently the doorbell would ring and Alice would go to the entry to make sure that her instructions were carried out; but close behind her would be William, exclaiming, "Come in! Come right in!"

HUMILITY

* JOKES *

The hardest thing about being humble is that you can't brag about it.

* QUOTATIONS *

Rudyard Kipling: Adam was a gardener, and God, who made him, sees that half of all good gardening is done upon the knees.

* * *

Neal A. Maxwell: The Duke of Wellington had a refrain, "I am but a man," which is not unlike the story of Washington riding through a small town and overhearing a girl of seven who had been brought out to see him, the hero, exclaim, "Why, he is only a man!" whereupon General Washington swept off his hat, bowed, and said, "Yes, miss, that's all I am."

Wellington, who was frequently plied with questions for years after his great victories, particularly the victory at Waterloo, reflected his humility even in his humor. Asked whether he'd had a particularly good view of the Battle of Waterloo, Wellington replied, "I generally like to see what I'm about." Another inquiry asked if he was "surprised at Waterloo." Wellington replied, "No, madam, but I am now!" (*Meek and Lowly,* 27).

* * *

Rudger Clawson: You see here on the pulpit a movable platform that can be raised up and let down to suit the speaker. It is not a Republican platform; it is not a Democratic platform; it is a Church platform and I can hardly reach up to it (Conference Report, Oct. 1940, 121).

* * *

Sterling W. Sill: In listening to this very generous introduction of Dr. Bernhard's, I thought of a man who said to his wife, "How many really great men do you think there are in the world?"

And she said, "I don't know, but I am sure of this: There is one less than you think there is" (*Speeches of the Year,* 21 Feb. 1962, 1).

111

* * *

Stephen L Richards: I lay aside the beautiful lei made of baby orchids, presented to us so graciously by our Hawaiian sisters, while I speak, fearing too sharp a contrast between the brilliance of its beauty, and the drabness of what may follow (*Improvement Era,* June 1957, 392).

* S T O R I E S *

John Tyler, president of the United States from 1841 to 1845, wrote the following inscription over the grave of his horse: "Here lies the body of my good horse, 'The General.' For twenty years he bore me around the circuit of my practice, and in all that time he never made a blunder. Would that his master could say the same!"

* * *

At a White House reception during the Civil War, one of the visitors shook the president's hand and told him solemnly that the future of the country depended on God and Abraham Lincoln.

"You are half right," responded the president.

* * *

During the war, General Dwight D. Eisenhower spoke to a group of soldiers. As he left the platform from which he was speaking, he slipped in the mud. The soldiers roared with laughter, causing Ike to comment later, "You know, of all the things I said and did to raise the morale of those troops, it was that fall on the seat of my pants which did them the most good."

* * *

In 1858, Abraham Lincoln was debating against Stephen A. Douglas, his opponent in a campaign for the U.S. Senate. Not only was Lincoln not as great an orator as Douglas, he was also not what one would call a handsome man. At one point Douglas accused Lincoln of being two-faced. Lincoln replied, "I leave it to my audience. If I had two faces, would I be wearing this one?"

* * *

An old acquaintance of President Lincoln visited him in Washington. Lincoln desired to give him an appointed office. Thus encouraged, the visitor, who was an honest man but wholly inexperienced in public affairs or business, asked for a high office, Superintendent of the Mint.

The President was aghast and said, "Good gracious! Why didn't he ask to be Secretary of the Treasury, and have done with it?"

Afterward, Lincoln said: "Well, now, I never thought Mr. _____ had anything more than average ability, when we were young men together. But, then, I suppose he thought the same thing about me— and here I am!"

* * *

J. Golden Kimball was thin, but after an illness he was even thinner than usual. Standing to address a congregation, he said in his high voice, "Can you hear me?"

No one responded.

He continued, "Can you see me?" (Cheney, *Golden Legacy*, 107).

* * *

General Dwight D. Eisenhower enjoyed telling the story of two soldiers who saw him in Europe when he was Supreme Allied Commander.

"How would you like his job?" one of the GIs asked.

"Not me," the other soldier replied. "No chance of promotion."

* * *

Spencer W. Kimball liked to tell this story about an experience that occurred after his call as a new, and therefore relatively unknown, General Authority. After a stake conference meeting, someone said to him, "You know, Elder Lee, I was glad you came to visit our stake, because I keep getting you confused with Brother Richards" (Kimball, "Spencer W. Kimball," *BYU Studies* 25[4]: 63).

* * *

After Spencer W. Kimball was called as an apostle, but before he had been sustained, he continued to serve as stake president. He wrote, "We went up early yesterday morning to Franklin for Sunday School and testimony meeting, then to Duncan for testimony meeting at 12:30, then up to Virden for 2:30 meeting. All the meetings started out as testimony meetings regular and ended in testimonials for me. I told the boys as we went late to the last two meetings that I was the first corpse I had ever seen that had three funerals in one day and was late for two of them. I needed only pallbearers and an open grave to make it complete" (adapted from Kimball, "Spencer W. Kimball," *BYU Studies* 25[4]: 63).

HYPOCRISY

* QUOTATIONS *

If you are going to be a hypocrite, at least be sincere about it.

* * *

J. Golden Kimball: Men come to me occasionally, not very often, and shake me by the hand and say, "I am glad to shake hands with a good man." I never feel so "cheap" as when that happens, and I have always been thankful that they did not know me so well as I know myself. . . .

What is a good man? That has been a big problem with me. I have had a good deal of business dealings with men who claimed to be good men. They said they were good and they told me how good they were, and when they got through with me I did not have anything left (Conference Report, Oct. 1932, 17).

* STORIES *

A bishop visited the home of one of his less active members.

"Why don't you come join us next Sunday?" the bishop said.

"I refuse to set foot in the door of that church. There are just too many hypocrites there."

"Oh, I wouldn't let that stop you," the bishop said, smiling. "There's always room for one more."

INDIVIDUAL WORTH

* JOKES *

Cashier (staring at customer's ID): You know, I have another customer with the same name as yours.

Customer: Really? Who?

* * *

I was so unpopular in high school that instead of being mentioned in the "Who's Who" section of the yearbook, I was listed under "Who's He?"

* * *

Two contented cows were grazing in a field when they looked up and saw a shiny, handsome milk truck drive out of the dairy lane. On the truck was painted:

FRESH MILK
pasteurized
homogenized
vitamin D added

One cow said, "Did you see that truck?"
"Yeah," mooed the other.
"Makes you feel pretty inadequate, doesn't it?"

* * *

A mother was teaching her young daughter about individual worth. "Everyone is a child of God," she said. "The children of God are everywhere!"
Puzzled, the daughter asked, "Then where are all the *adults* of God?"

* Q U O T A T I O N S *

Sharlene Wells Hawkes: I once gave a lesson to a Sunday School class of sixteen- and seventeen-year-olds on the topic of personal integrity, in which I asked this question: "What do you think the Lord would say if he were to make a short statement about you?" I passed around paper and pencils and asked the class members to write down an honest, soul-searching answer. They didn't have to sign their statements, and I hoped they would feel free to respond candidly. I should have known that when teenagers are given an opportunity to write whatever they want, and do so anonymously, well, it's as though they've just discovered "free speech."

The first response simply read, "Awesome." . . . Another student . . . had written, "One of his most favorite kids—a real good guy with a small ego." . . .

"Struggling to define her beliefs and values, but walking in the right direction," one student wrote. . . .

And my personal favorite: "He is a little confused, but he will straighten out" (Hawkes, *Living In but Not Of the World,* 87–88).

* * *

Mary Ellen Edmunds: Years ago I heard a story about a large family that went on a vacation. Mostly they bought food in grocery stores . . . to save money, but once in a while they went into a restaurant. They always caused quite a stir, as there were so many of them. . . .

On one such adventure they finally got seated and the waitress was taking their orders. She took a few orders and then got to a little boy around eleven years old. "And what would you like?" she asked. He looked over at his mother. After all, she usually chose for him. It was an awkward moment, but the mother didn't say anything, so he looked at the waitress and said, "I'll have a hot dog!"

At that moment his mother regained her voice and said, "Oh, no, he'll have what the rest of us are having." The waitress didn't seem to hear that comment and continued looking at the little boy. "What would you like on the hot dog?" He squirmed a bit and looked again at his mother. She once again seemed to lose her voice. So the little boy excitedly told the waitress what he wanted on the hot dog. . . . She wrote it down, took the rest of the orders, and left.

The little boy was amazed. He couldn't believe it. He turned to everyone else at the table and said, "She thinks I'm real!" (Edmunds, *Love Is a Verb,* 30–31).

* * *

Norma J. Ashton: Oliver Wendell Holmes was only about five feet tall. In a large meeting he was the shortest person in attendance. A man said to him, "Don't you feel strange being so short among all these taller men?" "Yes," Mr. Holmes replied, "I feel like a dime among pennies" ("The Joys of Testimony," *Joy*, 31).

* * *

The young daughter of William Howard Taft III was assigned to write a short autobiography, as was each child at the start of a new grade. Here's what she wrote: "My great-grandfather was President of the United States [27th President, 1909–13]. My grandfather [Robert Alphonso Taft, 1889–1953] was Senator from Ohio. My father is Ambassador to Ireland. I am a Brownie."

* STORIES *

When the Primary Children's Hospital was being built during the 1940s, the "Buy-a-Brick" campaign was one of the successful fund-raising drives. Each Primary child was asked to contribute ten cents to buy a brick for the hospital. The drive raised more than $20,000, which was used to buy 203,303 bricks and mortar.

At one time, a Primary board member was leading a tour of children through the finished building when a little boy asked her, "Lady, can you tell me which is my brick?" (see Madsen and Oman, *Sisters and Little Saints*, 130).

* * *

A family was giving a dinner party. Soon the adults of the family and their guests were engaged in animated conversation, to the complete exclusion of their four-year-old daughter. After a time the little girl tentatively plucked at her mother's sleeve and asked, "Remember me?"

INITIATIVE

* J O K E S *

A motorist got bogged down in the sticky clay of an unpaved Georgia road, and paid ten dollars to be pulled out by a Georgia cracker with a team of mules. "I should think," said the motorist, just about to get into his car to continue, "that you would be pulling people out of this stuff day and night."

"Nope," drawled the man, "at night's when we tote the water for the roads."

INTEGRITY

* Q U O T A T I O N S *

J. Golden Kimball: When I look over this body of men, I do not discover that you are very distinguished in appearance. Why, you are no better looking than I am, and I look pretty bad. . . . I am only a remnant of what I ought to be. I am not very well groomed, and I do not look distinguished; neither do you. . . . You can't boast very much about your appearance. We are a hard working people, and we would not take a very good picture, unless you take the better side of us: but I tell you, in the name of the Lord, we have got clean hearts; we love the Lord; we love truthfulness; we desire to be honest, truthful, and virtuous. You can't judge us by our appearance. If you knew the hearts of this people, there would not be the bitterness there is against the Latter-day Saints (Conference Report, Oct. 1910, 34).

119

Intentions

* QUOTATIONS *

ElRay L. Christiansen: "I think of a man they told me about in one of the stakes I was in not long ago. You know how we go out and try to activate the inactive, bring them along, get them to attend Church meetings while time lasts. A president of an elders' quorum told this story of a man whom they had called on many times, a good man who had good intentions. He welcomed them to his home, listened to them, and he would usually say, 'Well, I will. I intend to. I will do it. I will come to Church when I get straightened out.'

"Then they would go back another time, and he would give them the same story, 'Well, when I get straightened out, I'll come to Church.'

"Then the elders' president said, 'I was called on to speak at that man's funeral. He was in Church all right, and he was surely straightened out'" (*Speeches of the Year,* 14 Mar. 1962, 5–6).

Judging

* STORIES *

Two judges at a state fair couldn't decide which of two bulls should win the blue ribbon. Finally they picked a young boy from the crowd and asked him to pick the winner. After the awards ceremony, they asked the boy how he arrived at his decision.

"I just chose the one I thought would give the best milk," he said (see Nash, *Lengthen Your Smile,* 333).

JUDGMENT

* JOKES *

A Gospel Doctrine teacher was exhorting the class to prepare themselves so they might avoid the wrath that would be visited upon the unrighteous. "I warn you," he thundered, "there will be weeping and wailing and gnashing of teeth!"

At this moment an old woman stood up. "Brother Bowen," she exclaimed, "I have no teeth!"

"Sister Wendell," replied the teacher, "teeth will be provided!"

JUSTICE

* QUOTATIONS *

J. Golden Kimball: "I am not going to announce any blood and thunder doctrine to you today. I have not been radical for four long months, not since I had appendicitis. I came very nearly being operated upon. I thought I was going to die for a few hours. People said to me, "Why, brother Kimball, you needn't be afraid, you'll get Justice." "Well," I said, "that is what I am afraid of" (Conference Report, Oct. 1905, 81).

KINDNESS

* STORIES *

In a gloomy and depressed state, American writer Eugene Field wandered into a restaurant. A busy waiter hastened up and reeled off at high speed a long line of dishes on the menu. Field gazed up in melancholy and said, "Friend, I want none of these things. All I want is an orange and a few kind words."

KNOWLEDGE

* JOKES *

A young college student had stayed up all night studying for his zoology test the next day. As he entered the classroom, he saw ten stands with ten birds on them with a sack over each bird and only the legs showing. He sat right on the front row because he wanted to do the best job possible. The professor announced that the test would be to look at each of the birds' legs and give the common name, habitat, genus, species, and so on.

The student looked at the birds' legs. They all looked the same to him. He began to get upset. He had stayed up all night studying and now had to identify the birds by their legs. The more he thought about it the madder he got. Finally, he could stand it no longer. He went up to the professor's desk and said, "What a stupid test! How could anyone tell the difference between birds by looking at their legs?" With that the student threw his test on the professor's desk and walked to the door.

The professor was surprised. The class was so big that he didn't know every student's name, so as the student reached the door the professor called, "Wait, what's your name?"

The enraged student pulled up his pant legs and said, "You guess, buddy! You guess!"

* * *

In Primary one day, Sister Hanson asked Rob, a young sports fanatic, "Who defeated the Nephites?"

Rob's answer: "I dunno. If they don't play the Forty-niners, I don't keep track of them."

* * *

A teacher said, "Give me two personal pronouns," and she pointed to a certain child, who replied, "Who, me?"

* * *

Someone said about her friend, a Ph.D. candidate, "It seems to me that she's learning more and more about less and less, and I'm really afraid that by the time she has her degree she'll know everything about nothing."

* * *

Son: How did God make the world, Daddy?
Father: Hmmm, I don't know.
Son: What's heaven like?
Father: Well, I couldn't say.
Son: I'm not bothering you, am I, Daddy?
Father: Of course not. Why, you'll never learn anything if you don't ask questions!

* * *

A three-year-old girl used to reply to any statement made to her with, "I know." For example, "The world is round." ("I know.") "People should always tell the truth." ("I know.")

One day the girl's older brother said to her, "You always answer everything with 'I know.'"

"I know," answered the girl. "But what's wrong with that?"

"Well," said her brother, "only God knows everything!"

"I know."

* * *

The car simply would not run. The mechanic who was called in lifted the hood, reached inside, gave a twist of the wrist to a little mechanism—and all was well.

"What do I owe you?"

"One hundred and ten dollars," said the mechanic.

"Good heavens!" said the car owner. "That seems like an awful lot for just twisting a little gadget. How do you itemize it?"

"Well," said the mechanic, "ten dollars for twisting the little gadget. A hundred dollars for knowing which little gadget to twist."

* QUOTATIONS *

Charles W. Nibley: When a boy goes through the eighth grade and then the high school, then three or four years in a university, and then in a finishing off school, or something of that kind, the boy is twenty-five years old. There is a quarter of a century of his life spent in educating him. Somebody else has worked for the food he has eaten, and for the clothes that he has been supplied with for a full quarter of a century, which has been all spent in giving him education. He comes back home and he knows a lot; bless your soul, he can tell you pretty much about everything, but he doesn't know how to do scarcely anything (Conference Report, Apr. 1923, 148).

* * *

J. Golden Kimball: I am going to ask you a few questions, and will let you answer them. If you don't know enough to answer them, then you don't know as much as I do (Conference Report, Oct. 1917, 135).

* * *

Richard R. Lyman: I had a little pamphlet put in my hands the other day, and in it is a story something like this: ("It is up to You," by Parlette.) A newspaper man in a paper mill was watching the operations of a machine with interest, when along came a man with an oil can, squirting oil into the squirt holes in the side of the machine. He asked that man a few questions that he answered fairly well. Then he asked something about the process going on in the next room, and the man replied: "I don't know nothing about it, boss, I haven't worked there." So he said he asked him another process and the answer came the same: "I don't know nothing about it, boss, I haven't worked there." He asked him a question about the pulp mill: "I don't know nothing about it, boss, I have never worked there." He asked him a question about the office, the number of people employed in the plant: "I don't know nothing about it, boss, I haven't worked there." And so the newspaper man, to himself, said: "Nobody home."

The newspaper man asked: "I presume, my friend, that you are new in this plant?" "No, no," came the reply, "I have been squirting oil into this machine now for twelve years." Twelve years and "don't know nothing" about any other part of the institution. He said: "I took off my hat in the presence of the dead."

As he was leaving he asked the foreman: "You see that man standing over there with a can in his hand? Is he a human being, or do you just wind him up?" (Conference Report, Oct. 1921, 105–6).

* * *

Addison Everett: At Coleville, [Joseph Smith] and Oliver [Cowdery] were under arrest on a charge of deceiving the people. When they were at the justice's house for trial in the evening, all were waiting for Mr. Reid, Joseph's lawyer. And while waiting, the justice asked Joseph some questions, among which was this: "What was the first miracle Jesus performed?" Joseph replied, "He made this world, and what followed we are not told" (*Young Woman's Journal*, Oct. 1890, 75–76).

* STORIES *

William Lyon Phelps, on a pre-Christmas examination paper, found written, "God only knows the answer to this question. Merry Christmas."

He returned the paper with the notation, "God gets an A; you get an F. Happy New Year."

* * *

The philosopher Aristotle was once asked how educated men were superior to those uneducated. His answer: "As much as the living are to the dead."

* * *

A lad once asked Mozart how to write a symphony. Mozart said, "You're a very young man. Why not begin with ballads?"

The aspiring young boy urged, "You composed symphonies when you were ten years old."

"Yes," replied Mozart, "but I didn't ask how."

* * *

Lincoln was told of a profound historian, "It may be doubted whether any man of our generation has plunged more deeply into the sacred fount of learning."

"Yes, or come up drier," said Lincoln.

LAST DAYS

* J O K E S *

The editor of a tiny, small-town newspaper had cherished for many years a set of gigantic old-fashioned wooden type. His assistants had often tried to get him to use it, but he always firmly vetoed the idea.

One summer the old man went away for a fishing trip. In his absence a cyclone struck the town, tore the steeple off the church, unroofed several houses, sucked a couple of wells dry, and scattered a few barns around.

No bigger calamity had hit the town in years. So, figuring "now's our chance," his assistants got down the giant type from the shelf and set up a sensational front-page headline with it.

Two days later the editor came storming into the office. "Balls of fire!" he shouted. "What do you mean by taking down that type for a cyclone? All these years I've been saving it for the end of the world!"

* Q U O T A T I O N S *

Brigham Young: I would like to see the footsteps of the Almighty (and they are now beginning to be visible) in his going forth to cut off the bitter branches; and by-and-bye the stone cut out of the mountain will begin to roll, and if it does not soon crush some of the toes of the great image, I am mistaken. From present appearances I think the toes will be pretty well mutilated before the stone reaches them (*Journal of Discourses* 9:273–74).

LEADERSHIP

* JOKES *

A bishop of a small, struggling ward in a small town had the odd habit of rushing over to the train tracks every day to watch the daily train pass by. One day several ward members came up to him and said, "Bishop, we think it's a little odd that you have this habit of watching trains. We've noticed that every day you leave your chores, drop whatever you're doing, and rush over here to watch that train. Don't you think that fascination with the railroad is a little juvenile for a man of your age and responsibilities?"

"Well, brothers," the bishop said, "I lead the ward, settle neighborhood arguments, spearhead community causes, head up the fund raising for the Scouts, and even call on people for the yearly Church magazine drive. No, I won't give up seeing that Western Pacific train every day. It's the only thing in this whole town I don't have to push!"

* * *

A self-important man was made foreman of the construction job where he worked. His first act was to fire one of his fellow-workers. "Why'd you do that?" one of the other workers asked. "What did you have against him?"

128

The foreman replied, "Oh, I didn't fire him because I had anything against him. I fired him because I had the authority."

* * *

Woman (on telephone with highway patrol office): Are the roads safe today, with the snow storm and everything?
Officer: They're slippery but passable.
Woman: I don't want to pass anyone, sir. I just want to know—is it safe to follow?

* QUOTATIONS *

Brigham Young: To guide the minds of the people and to govern and control them is a greater miracle than to raise the dead (*Journal of Discourses* 13:32–34).

* STORIES *

When George V was Prince of Wales, he held the rank of Lieutenant in the Marines. One day on the afterdeck of a battleship he was conducting drill under the supervision of a senior officer. The deck had been cleared even of its quadrails. The Prince was not well versed in drill and his superior was clearly put out at his awkwardness and slowness of command. At last the squad was marching full on for the stern and the unguarded edge and it seemed as though the Prince had either forgotten the command to stop, or face about, or else failed to realize the situation. As the men neared the edge, the officer snapped, "Good grief, sir, can't you at least say good-bye to your men?"

* * *

Willard L. Jones, a stake president in Nevada in the early 1900s, was a fast runner. One night he heard some noise in his melon patch and looked out to see several boys—all members of his ward—stealing watermelons.

When he stepped outside, the boys ran. The stake president was hot on their heels, but he wasn't fast enough to catch them.

The next day he passed one of the boys on his way to town. He tipped his hat, grinned, and said, "Nice run we had last night!" (adapted from *The Fighting Parson,* quoted in *Ensign,* May 1994, 48).

*   *   *

Shortly after having been sustained as President of the Church, a weary Spencer W. Kimball joked with his family, "If I had known it was going to be like this, I would never have run for the office" (see Kimball and Kimball, *Spencer W. Kimball,* 412).

*   *   *

An acquaintance once asked Abraham Lincoln, "You seem like a simple man. Don't you sometimes find the presidency, with all its trappings and ceremonies, rather tiresome?"

"Yes," Lincoln replied, "sometimes. In fact, I feel sometimes like a man who was ridden out of town on a rail, and said: 'If it wasn't for the honor of the thing, I'd rather walk!'"

LOVE

* **STORIES** *

In 1921 Elder David O. McKay, then a member of the Quorum of the Twelve, made a round-the-world trip. In a small New Zealand village he was met by a joyous audience of Latter-day Saints who gathered to greet him before a conference meeting. Elder McKay recorded in his journal, "From what we had read we knew we ought to do something . . . in response to this cordial, impassioned welcome; but we are an ignorant set of *pakehas*, so we stand and await instructions.

"Soon, Brother Christy suggests that instead of our making speeches, we are asked to shake hands with the multitude. . . . Being pretty well-filled with the Maori spirit, we found ourselves not only shaking hands, but *Hongi-ing* one by one (rubbing noses) and one after another, the several hundred people in line. . . .

"What an experience!" Elder McKay continued. "You who think Maori noses are all alike, have never *hongied* a multitude!" (see Llewelyn R. McKay, comp., *Home Memories of President David O. McKay*, 63).

* * *

President Abraham Lincoln once dropped a few kind words about the Confederates. A woman asked him how he could speak kindly of his enemies when he should rather destroy them.

"What, Madam, do I not destroy them when I make them my friends?"

* * *

On one occasion Spencer W. Kimball's sister Alice greeted him with a kiss and then said hello to others in the room. When she got back around to Brother Kimball, she said, "Did I kiss you already?" He replied, "The first time must not have impressed you very much" (Kimball, "Spencer W. Kimball," *BYU Studies* 25[4]: 69).

LOYALTY

* QUOTATIONS *

David O. McKay: I have rejoiced time and again, when visiting the different stakes surrounding Utah, to hear our brethren tell about the advantages of some particular town. "Why," they would say, for example, "we are blest with the purest air, we have the best water that can be found in the world;" and they will enumerate, one after another, the benefits and blessings of that particular locality. I recall now how the brethren in Canada were eager to impress those who were with them with the resources of that country. Why, the advantages were innumerable. For example, when one visitor said, "But you haven't the scenery we have in Utah." "Yes, we have," persisted President Wood; "we have even better scenery than you have in Utah." "Where?" " . . . I will show you;" and then a ride forty miles from Cardston took us to one of the most beautiful mountain scenes in the world—the Switzerland of America. He felt that there was nothing that could make him feel dissatisfied with his home there. "Even the winds in Canada," he said, "are blessing us, because they blow the snow off, so the cattle can eat the grass" (Conference Report, Apr. 1910, 107).

* STORIES *

During a time when his entire cabinet except for one member was against him, Abraham Lincoln told the story of a man at the Illinois revival meeting who slept when the preacher asked, "Who are on the Lord's side?" and the whole congregation except himself arose. The preacher then asked, "Who are on the side of the devil?" The man awoke, arose, and standing there alone, called out, "I don't exactly understand the question, but I'll stand by you, parson, to the last. But it seems to me that we're in a hopeless minority."

LYING

* QUOTATIONS *

Humorist Bill Nye about liars: "We have nothing more to say of the editor of the *Sweetwater Gazette*. Aside from the fact that he is a squint-eyed, consumptive liar, with a breath like a buzzard and a record like a convict, we don't know anything against him. He means well enough, and if he can evade the penitentiary and the vigilance committee for a few more years, there is a chance for him to end his life in a natural way. If he don't tell the truth a little more plentifully, however, the Green River people will rise as one man and churn him up till there won't be anything left of him but a pair of suspenders and a wart."

MANNERS

* JOKES *

As a young student entered her classroom, the teacher noticed his hands were dirty. She stopped him and said, "John, please wash your hands. My goodness, what would you say if I came into the room with hands like that?"

"Oh," the boy replied, "I think I'd be too polite to mention it."

* * *

Mother: Sam, I expect you to behave yourself here in your own home! What would your Scoutmaster say if you acted like that in Scout meeting?

Sam: He'd say, "Behave yourself, Sam—remember you're not at home now!"

* * *

Little Zachary had been to a birthday party, and when he got back home, his mother asked him questions about his manners at the party. "You didn't ask for a second piece of cake, did you?" she said.

"No, Mom," Zachary answered. "I just asked Jessica's mother for the recipe so that you could make some cake like it because it was the very best cake I'd ever tasted in my whole life. And she *gave* me another piece, of her own free will."

MARRIAGE

* J O K E S *

Eve: Adam, do you love me?
Adam: Who else?

* * *

"I've made up my mind what we'll call the baby," a young mother announced to her husband. "We'll call her Eulalia."

The father didn't like the name and he quickly thought of a solution. "That's fine," he said. "The first girl I loved was named Eulalia, and it will bring back pleasant memories."

The wife was silent for a moment. "We'll call her Mary after my mother," she said.

* * *

You can always tell when a marriage is on the rocks. The husband and wife don't even talk to each other during television commercials.

* * *

First gossip: I don't think the Joneses' son was ready for marriage.
Second gossip: Why do you say that?
First gossip: I went to the wedding reception, and the groom cried for two hours because the bride got a bigger piece of cake than he did!

* * *

A young couple had argued, and later as they drove through the countryside they saw a donkey standing in a field. "Are you related?" the man asked his wife, nodding toward the animal. "Not by blood," said the wife. "Only by marriage."

* * *

The golden-wedding celebration was over, and the family was listening as Mom talked radiantly about what the day had meant to her. As she tried to express her feelings, Dad cut in: "Well, now, I promised that if you married me, something nice would happen."

* * *

Mary: Dear, I'm crushed! You forgot my birthday!
Harry: But, sweetheart, how can you expect me to remember it when you keep looking younger every day?

* * *

Although usually not given to romantic impulses, a young man decided to stop on his way home from work and pick up a dozen roses and a box of candy for his wife. When he presented them to his sweetheart, she burst into tears. "This has been the worst day of my life," she sobbed. "The baby fell down the stairs, the phone has rung off the hook, I burned the meatloaf, and the toilet is plugged. And to top it all off, you've started drinking!"

* * *

Brother Johnson: Bishop, it's my wife's tidiness. It's driving me crazy!

Bishop: I'm surprised at you, Brother Johnson. Don't we teach that cleanliness is next to godliness?

Brother Johnson: Yes, Bishop. But if I drop my socks on the floor, she puts them in the laundry basket. If I throw my shirt on the chair, she hangs it up. The other night I couldn't sleep so I got up at three A.M. and went into the kitchen to get a glass of water. When I came back to the bedroom, the bed was made.

* * *

Brother Hatch: I think my marriage is deteriorating, Bishop.

Bishop: Why do you say that?

Brother Hatch: The other night I had a quarrel with my dog, and my wife said the dog was right.

* * *

An elderly Mormon woman accompanied her husband to the doctor's office. After his checkup, the doctor called the wife into his office alone.

"Your husband is suffering from a severe disease and horrible stress," he said. "But you can prolong his life if you'll do a few simple things."

"What do I have to do?"

"Each morning, fix him a healthy breakfast. Be pleasant, and always treat him with deference. Fix him just what he likes for lunch and dinner. Don't ask him to do any chores around the house—it will be too much of a burden to him. And don't discuss your problems with him; that will only make his stress worse. Most important, be loving and romantic with him several times a week and satisfy his every whim. If you can do this faithfully for the next year, I think your husband will regain his health completely."

The drive home was rather silent. Finally the husband turned to his wife and asked, "I have to know; what did the doctor say?"

The wife thought for a moment and then replied, "You're going to die."

* **P O E M S** *

Miss Nanny, A Little Pettikiller, Though Not Hard to Please
I do not like a man that's fat—
A man that's lean is worse than that;
Nor do I like a man that's tall—
A man that's little, is worse than all;
Nor do I like a man that's fair—
A man that's dark I cannot bear;
A young man is a constant pest—
An old man would my hours invest;
A man of sense I could not rule—
And yet I could not love a fool;
A sober man I will not take—
A drunken man my heart would break.
Man's face half shaved I hate to see.
But worse than all a great goatee.
All things I most sincerely hate,
And yet I love the married state.
(*Deseret News*, 13 July 1850; quoted in
Davis Bitton, *Wit and Whimsy in Mormon
History*, 23).

* * *

Wife: You're hopeless, dear. All you ever talk about is baseball!
Husband: Hah! You're way off base! Clear out in left field!

* Q U O T A T I O N S *

David O. McKay: It is said that during courtship we should keep our eyes wide open, but after marriage keep them half-shut.

What I mean may be illustrated by a young woman who said to her husband, "I know that my cooking isn't good; I hate it as much as you do, but do you find me sitting around griping about it?" (Conference Report, Apr. 1956, 8–9).

* * *

Orson Hyde: There are many living now who are bachelors. I do not complain of the very old men, for they cannot help themselves at all times, but I am going to complain of the old bachelors; and I tell you what it is, if you do not step forward and marry, and try to carry on the great work of Jehovah, it will be left for a better man to do than you. [Voice in the stand, "There is but one old bachelor in the Territory, and he has gone to the States."] O! I beg your pardon; President Young says he does not know of but one old bachelor in all the Territory of Utah, and he has gone to the States; therefore I have nothing more to say on this particular point (*Journal of Discourses* 2:84).

* * *

Charles W. Nibley: I stood at my window, only the other day, and watched a couple going down the street—a big, strong young fellow and his wife, a beautiful woman, tagging behind him. I thought, "They are married, all right." If he had not been, why he would have had hold of her arm, showing her a little attention and courtesy, and I felt like I would like to go out there and kick that fellow (Conference Report, Apr. 1924, 48).

* * *

George Albert Smith: You know, when I was growing up I never saw a difference of opinion between my father and my mother. I used to think that was a miracle, and after I had been married for twenty years, I knew it was a miracle (in *BYU Speeches of the Year*, 1961, 5).

* * *

Reed Smoot: I have never left my home, when my wife was there, from the day that I had a home, up till this very morning, without kissing my wife goodbye. I never left her at noon-time, in my life, unless I kissed her goodbye. And I wish that every Latter-day Saint would follow this practice—not to kiss my wife, but his own (Conference Report, Oct. 1909, 72).

* * *

Hugh B. Brown: We are reminded of the young bride who, on her wedding day, said to her mother, "I am the happiest girl in the world. I have come to the end of all my troubles."

And the wise mother replied, "Yes my dear, but you don't know which end" (Conference Report, Apr. 1963, 6–7).

* STORIES *

Bruce R. McConkie and his wife were talking one night about the many blessings membership in the Church had brought into their lives. Finally, Sister McConkie asked her husband to name his greatest blessing.

"Without a moment's hesitation," said Elder McConkie, "I said, 'The greatest blessing that has ever come to me was on the 13th day of October in 1937 at 11:20 A.M. when I was privileged to kneel in the Salt Lake Temple at the Lord's altar and receive you as an eternal companion.'"

"Well," replied his wife, "you passed that test" (see *New Era*, January 1975, 38).

* * *

When Joseph Fielding Smith and Jessie Evans were married in the Salt Lake Temple, President Heber J. Grant said at the conclusion of the ceremony, "Now, Joseph, kiss your wife." President Smith referred to that directive in an interview on their thirty-third wedding anniversary [in] 1971, commenting, "He said it like he meant it, and I have been doing it ever since" (Swinton, *In the Company of Prophets*, 61–62).

* * *

Years ago Elder Spencer W. Kimball, then a member of the Quorum of the Twelve, was visiting with a young man who was just about to complete his full-time missionary service. "When you get released, Elder," said Elder Kimball, "What are your plans?"

"Oh, I plan to go back to college," said the elder, "then I hope to fall in love and get married."

Elder Kimball offered this wise counsel: "Well, don't just pray to marry the one you love," said the apostle. "Instead, pray to love the one you marry" (see Joe J. Christensen, "Marriage and the Great Plan of Happiness," *Ensign*, May 1995, 64).

* * *

Spencer W. Kimball and his wife, Camilla, had a good relationship, but they occasionally had minor differences. Once they attended a party for another couple who were celebrating their golden wedding anniversary. When the speaker said the couple had never raised their voices at each other, Spencer whispered to a friend, "It must have been dull" (Kimball, "Spencer W. Kimball," *BYU Studies* 25[4]: 61).

MEETINGS

* J O K E S *

If all the people who sleep in church were laid end to end, they'd be a lot more comfortable.

* * *

The 14th Article of Faith:

14. We believe in meetings—all that have been scheduled, all that are now scheduled, and we believe that there will yet be many more great and important meetings. We have endured many meetings and hope to be able to endure all meetings. If there is a meeting, we seek after it.

* Q U O T A T I O N S *

Nicholas G. Smith: All my life I have looked with the spirit of reverence upon this building. I never dreamed that one day I should be privileged to sit upon these red plush seats. Since living within a stone's throw of Temple Block, my mother was always anxious that we attend the two o'clock afternoon session each Sunday, and as a boy I used to say:

"Mother, it does not do any good for me to go over there, I just go to sleep. I cannot stay awake in the Tabernacle."

"Well, son, that shows there's a good spirit there. . . . There is nothing to be afraid of, and I want you to go" (Conference Report, Oct. 1941, 63).

* * *

J. Golden Kimball: I remember a long time ago when the Mutuals launched the *Era*. I was on a trip with Apostle Francis M. Lyman—we started in at Sevier and went to Panguitch and the surrounding settlements and to Kanab and St. George; and when we got to St. George, Brother David H. Cannon, the President of the Stake, and Brother Edward Snow, superintendent of the Mutuals, with their buggies transferred us to Panacca. The people had not seen an Apostle for twenty years, and it was Sunday, a fast day. Meetings were begun in the morning and they kept them up all day, and we were fasting. I was pretty nearly dead at four o'clock. After four o'clock Brother Lyman said, "Now, Brother Kimball, get up and tell them about the *Era*." He had done a good deal of talking himself about the *Era*. . . . So I [got up] and I said: "All you men that will take the *Era* if we will let you go home, raise your right hand." There was not a single man who did not raise his hand and subscribed and paid $2.00 cash for the *Era*. . . . Brother Lyman said: "That is the brightest thing you ever did." I do not claim that was inspiration; it was good psychology. Really they paid $2.00 to get out (Conference Report, Apr. 1932, 78).

* * *

Brigham Young: If you can make as good a beginning as did an old lady, you will do well. She went to a schoolhouse, and, on her return, called at a neighbor's who inquired where she had been. She replied, "I have been to meeting." "Has there been a meeting?" "Oh, yes, and a glorious one, too." "Dear me, we did not hear of it. Were there many there?" "No, there were not many." "Who was there?" "Why, the Lord was there, and I was there, and had a blessed good meeting." If you cannot get any person to meet with you, be sure and have the Lord meet with you, and you will soon gain confidence in yourselves and have influence with your brethren (*Journal of Discourses* 8:65).

* S T O R I E S *

At a meeting of General Authorities, President Spencer W.
Kimball, his eyesight nearly gone, said, "Brethren, I'm sorry I can't
see you, but I assume you're here" (Kimball, "Spencer W. Kimball,"
BYU Studies 25[4]: 69).

* * *

An unknown pioneer told this story: "The Old Tabernacle that
formerly occupied the present site of the handsome new Assembly
Hall was once the scene of a most inglorious episode in my life, which
I am frequently reminded of when I see any of those who, as my
youthful companions, were present on the occasion.

"On a sultry summer afternoon a half dozen or more playful
boys, myself among the number, occupied one of the seats in that
building farthest removed from the speaker. On the seat immediately
in front of [us] sat a man on whom the preacher's discourse or the
hot weather, or both, seemed to have rather a somnolent effect. With
his head leaned backward and his mouth open, he slept, while his
breath came and went in fitful snatches and small explosions. He was
soon the center of attraction for quite an extended circle of interested, if not admiring, auditors. The nervous ladies in the vicinity
doubtless eyed him with a good deal of concern, as the agonized manner of his breathing probably led them to expect that every succeed-
ing hitch in his breath would be a permanent one. The boys found
amusement in watching his snoring struggles, while the pious old
men, anxious to hear the preaching, looked daggers at him for creat-
ing such a disturbance. All at once an idea occurred to a large boy on
the end of the seat behind him, who, by the way, was a great practical
joker. Drawing from his pocket a long lead pencil, he passed it along
the row of boys to where I sat, behind the sleeper, and motioned for
me to tickle him with it. The other boys also immediately joined in

urging me to do it as an excellent joke, and entering into the spirit of the fun, I assented. Reaching over with the pencil, I tickled him about the ear, causing him to wake up with a snort, and all the boys to laugh.

"In a few moments, however, our drowsy neighbor apparently lapsed into another doze. I say *apparently*, for I believed afterwards that he was only feigning sleep—throwing out a little chaff to catch the birds who were annoying him, which I was silly enough to mistake for real grain.

"Flattered with my success the first time, and the encouragement I received from the other boys, I tried the tickling process again, when lo! to my surprise and chagrin, he whirled, as I was in the act, and struck me a blow over the head.

"I looked at the boys, and saw that they were nearly convulsed with laughter at my expense, and then I looked at the man, and felt as if I would like to do something desperate. But then it was a place of worship, and besides he was much older and stronger than I was, and discretion forbade my retaliating there. The boys prevented me from hitting him with a cobble stone as he emerged from the door after the service was closed, and by the time I next saw the man my anger had worn off and I had concluded that he served me right.

"I learned a lesson by my experience that day, in fact two or three of them.

"I learned that when a sleepy man is tickled in meeting, no matter who the instigators are, if he has spirit enough to resent it, it is generally the fellow at the other end of the pencil who has to suffer the consequences.

"I learned that when a person indulges in any foolishness for the sake of affording amusement to jovial or thoughtless companions, he can't count with any certainty on their sympathy when his acts lead him into trouble. Laughter is cheap, and they can afford to indulge in it while their heads are in no danger.

"I learned that a house of worship is not exactly the place to play practical jokes in.

"I learned that there are other ways (and more congenial ways at least to one party) of waking a sleeping man in meeting than getting a small boy to tickle him about the ear with a pencil.

"The joker who handed me the pencil is now a prominent and portly bishop in our Church, and I—well, I think I am a little wiser if not better than when I used that pencil" (*Juvenile Instructor,* 15 Mar. 1880).

* * *

Once J. Golden Kimball was assigned to conduct the sustaining of Church officers during a stake conference. "It has been proposed," he began, "that we sustain Brother Heber J. Grant as prophet, seer, and revelator of The Church of Jesus Christ of Latter-day Saints. All in favor make it manifest by the raising of the right hand; opposed, if any, by the same sign. . . . It has been proposed that we sustain Brother Anthony W. Ivins as . . ." And so on. After a while, Brother Kimball looked up from his list and noticed that the congregation was nodding off. So in a monotonous tone he continued, "It has been proposed that Mount Nebo be moved from its present site in Juab County and be placed on the Utah-Idaho border. All in favor make it manifest by raising the right hand; opposed, by the same sign." The few who were still awake began to chuckle, reviving the congregation (Fife and Fife, *Saints of Sage and Saddle,* 305).

MEMORY

MEMORY

* QUOTATIONS *

Orson F. Whitney: I heard a story of a . . . gentleman who possessed a phenomenal memory. He was the keeper of the cloak room at a fashionable hotel, and his memory served him so faithfully, that he was not under the necessity of using checks when the guests left with him their hats or coats or canes. When they returned for them, he never failed to give each man his own. A certain judge went to that hotel for the special purpose of testing this man's marvelous memory. He gave him his hat—a hundred others did likewise—and passed into the dining room. Returning in about an hour, sure enough, he got the right hat back again. "Well," he exclaimed, "that is remarkable. How did you know that was my hat?" "I don't know that that is your hat, judge," said the keeper. "Well, why did you give it to me, then?" "Because you gave it to me" (Conference Report, Oct. 1919, 68).

MIRACLES

* QUOTATIONS *

Orson F. Whitney: In the Eighteenth Ward, one Sunday evening, a Primary Conference was held, at which one of the sisters, gathering a class of little children around her, related to them how the Savior fed the multitude—fed five thousand people, with five loaves of bread and two fishes. Going home, a mother asked her little son what he had heard, and he repeated, as best he could, the teacher's instructions. The mother, anxious to impress the lesson upon the mind of her child, asked: "How, do you suppose, did the Savior feed five thousand people with five loaves of bread and two fishes?" The little boy thought a moment, and then said: "Well, I don't believe those in the middle got any" (Conference Report, Apr. 1911, 50).

MISSIONARY WORK

* J O K E S *

Two missionaries who had been out tracting all day knocked on yet another door. When the lady of the house answered, she took one look at them and slammed the door. Tired of being rejected, the missionaries decided to try something new. They ran around to the back door and knocked. The same woman answered, but before she could slam the door again, the elders said, "Boy! We hope you're not as mean as the lady in front!"

* * *

When Elder Johnson was set apart by his stake president, his longtime girlfriend dissolved into tears. "Don't worry," the stake president said, trying to console her. "I'll let you kiss him good-bye."

The young woman cheered up immediately. "You will? How many times?"

* * *

Two missionaries were walking down a country road when a huge, angry dog emerged from a field not far from them. One of the elders immediately grabbed his sneakers from his backpack and bent over to put them on. His companion watched with astonishment. "What are you doing? You'll never outrun that dog!"

The first elder finished tying his shoes and stood up. "I don't have to run faster than the *dog*," he said. "I just have to run faster than you!"

* * *

Sometimes I wake up Grumpy on P-day, but sometimes I let my companion sleep in.

* * *

Elder Timms loved to cook—but his meals often left much to be desired. One day his companion came into the kitchen and saw him crying as he heated a pan of soup.

"What's the matter, Elder? Bad news from home? A 'Dear John'?"

"No, it's worse! I made some meatloaf for our dinner tonight, but the neighbor's cat ate the whole thing."

"It's okay, Elder. We can get her another one."

* QUOTATIONS *

William W. Seegmiller: I am one of the derelict to whom Elder Thomas E. McKay referred when he inferred that some of the mission presidents in reporting their labors to the Quorum of the Twelve, did not pay due recognition and homage to the services of their wives. In a spirit of penitence I now undertake to make proper restitution.

The other day I was seeking the home of a returned Brazilian missionary. I found the number and rang the bell. A lady came to the door with that indifferent expression on her face—you know what I mean. . . . I said: "I am President Seegmiller of the Brazilian Mission." She said: "Oh, President Seegmiller, our son loves you so much, especially Sister Seegmiller." . . . There are parents of 500 missionaries who feel the same way. So it seems to me that my puny efforts at expressing my appreciation of my missionary companion are all unnecessary (Conference Report, Oct. 1945, 146).

* * *

J. Golden Kimball: I remember when we arrived at Chattanooga, Brother Roberts sent me and a son of an apostle into Virginia. When our visit in Chattanooga was over, and we had paid our expenses I had ten dollars. When we got to the end of the railroad I said to my companion: "Let's ride in a carriage, it will be the last time we will ever see one." I did not know that I was a prophet, but it came true. When we reached our field of labor we lay around there for about three weeks. I said to my companion, who was from the Brigham Young Academy, "Let us go up into the woods and see if we can sing," (I couldn't carry a tune, I never tried to sing in the Academy), "and let us go up and learn to pray." We did not have any audience, only those great big trees. And I said "Let us learn to preach." I would advise young elders to do that before they start out and not practice so much on the people; we practiced on the trees. So I prepared myself and occupied the time. My companion was prepared, and we sang. We made an awful mess of it, but after a while—and that is another testimony— God brought the tunes to us, and we could sing the songs that we had listened to in the Academy. Then I preached. God was kind to us and he loosed our tongues and we found we were able to express the things we had studied. I remember my companion was dismissing. We had our eyes shut and our hands up. I thought he would never get through; and when he said, Amen, we looked back, and there were four men standing behind us with guns on their shoulders. I said to my companion, "That is another lesson, from this time on in the South; I shall pray with one eye open" (Conference Report, Oct. 1925, 158).

* * *

J. Golden Kimball: I have never been ashamed to testify to the divinity of this work, when I felt that I had the Spirit of God. I have held the name of the Prophet Joseph Smith as sacred. When I was in the mission field, I said to the Elders: whenever you are moved upon by the Spirit of God, and; the spirit of testimony, you are to testify that Joseph Smith is a Prophet of God, and I promise you it will make you all the trouble you can bear (Conference Report, Apr. 1908, 115).

* * *

Brigham Young: Some Elders have in a manner to convey the idea that the practical part of our religion is only manifest here. We should be sorry if this were the case, and a little reflection will show them their mistake. Did you ever have sore feet and aching limbs, while travelling abroad preaching the Gospel? "Yes." Was that practical, or was it only spiritual? After walking twenty-five miles to fill an appointment, and, before eating a mouthful of food, preaching an hour or two, for nobody had thought you wanted anything to eat, and then baptising, and then wading through the mud for miles in wet clothes before you could get a dry sock, was that practical? I thought preaching the Gospel was as nigh manual labour as anything I could work at (*Journal of Discourses* 9:285).

* * *

Matthew Cowley: I was just turning seventeen when I was called to go to New Zealand as a missionary. My first appointment there was to a little place called Judea. . . . At the first meeting I attended in Judea, I could not understand the words that were being said, and after the meeting a sister who could speak English said to me: "Do you know what they said in there, and what they did?" I said: "I could not understand a word."

She said: "Well, you were called and sustained as the secretary of the Relief Society of the Judea Branch."

I made up my mind right there and then . . . to get the gift of the

Maori language, even if I had to work for it, and I did have to work for it (*Matthew Cowley Speaks*, 2).

* * *

Ted E. Brewerton: Why is Floriano Oliveira, a member of the high council in a stake in Brazil, so successful as a missionary? Because he *obeyed* the Lord's counsel to open his mouth and share the gospel. One day as he was driving through the congested traffic of São Paulo he took his eyes off the road for but a second and crashed into the car in front of him. He jumped out of the vehicle, hurried up to the car he had hit, opened the door and said, "I am so sorry I hit you. It was all my fault. I accept the full blame and will pay the total costs. I had no intention to do this, so please forgive me. Yet if I hadn't hit you, you wouldn't have received this message I have for you, the message that you have waited for all your life." He then explained the restoration of the gospel to the man, who was a medical doctor, and the man joined the Church two weeks later (*Ensign*, May 1981, 69).

* **S T O R I E S** *

Once two elders were tracting in the back country of the Ozarks. As they left one elderly couple, they overheard the man saying to his wife, "Ain't that a hoot, Maude! Both them boys named Elmer!"

* * *

When the Missionary Training Center was built in Provo, the Church planted beautiful green athletic fields right across the street so the missionaries would have a place to exercise. But the new grass was so inviting that BYU students liked to go there to play football, throw frisbees, or just lie around. When the missionaries went out, little room was left for their activities. The leaders of the MTC finally posted a large sign on the field: "Missionaries Only."

The next day, BYU students were out again in full force, playing their football and throwing frisbees on the field. Next to the official sign they had posted a new one: "Every member a missionary."

* * *

When J. Golden Kimball was serving as a full-time missionary in the Southern States Mission, two fellow missionaries were arrested and jailed. Elder Kimball later said, "The people from far and near, hearing of Mormon elders being under arrest, gathered to see these peculiar individuals. The brethren sang hymns and testified of the truth of the gospel, etc. It is claimed they had congregations of three hundred, and I have been told that the people had never heard such wonderful preaching and singing. The elders almost regretted getting their freedom. So, I am almost inclined to advocate putting our elders in jail once in a while, when they are unable to get a hearing in any other way" (see Cheney, *Golden Legacy*, 24–25).

* * *

At the age of thirty-seven, David Lawrence McKay, father of David O. McKay, received a mission call to Scotland. His wife, Jennette Evans McKay, was expecting a baby; the couple had three young children; and their farm and livestock operation required constant work from both husband and wife. David showed some hesitancy to accept the call at first, although Jennette immediately supported it.

David consulted with some of the brethren in his ward. Many of them agreed with David that his responsibilities were too great and that he should not accept the call. But his uncle, John Grow, offered wise counsel that David followed: "You may be right and you may be wrong," his uncle said, "but if Jennette has set her mind that you should answer the mission call, you might as well give in!" (Gibbons, *David O. McKay*, 10–11).

* * *

Parley P. Pratt: I was soon ordered to prison, or to pay a sum of money which I had not in the world. It was now a late hour, and I was still retained in court, tantalized, abused and urged to settle the matter, to all of which I made no reply for some time. This greatly exhausted their patience. It was near midnight. I now called on Brother Petersen to sing a hymn in the court. We sung, "O how happy are they." This exasperated them still more, and they pressed us greatly to settle the business, by paying the money.

I then observed as follows: "May it please the court, I have one proposal to make for a final settlement of the things that seem to trouble you. It is this: if the witnesses who have given testimony in the case will repent of their false swearing, and the magistrate of his unjust and wicked judgment and of his persecution, blackguardism and abuse, and all kneel down together, we will pray for you, that God might forgive you in these matters."

"My big bull dog pray for me," says that Judge.

"The devil help us," exclaimed another.

They now urged me for some time to pay the money; but got no further answer.

The court adjourned, and I was conducted to a public house over the way, and locked in till morning; the prison being some miles distant.

In the morning the officer appeared and took me to breakfast; this over, we sat waiting in the inn for all things to be ready to conduct me to prison. In the meantime my fellow travellers came past on their journey, and called to see me. I told them in an undertone to pursue their journey and leave me to manage my own affairs, promising to overtake them soon. They did so.

After sitting awhile by the fire in charge of the officer, I requested to step out. I walked out into the public square accompanied by him. Said I, "Mr. Peabody, are you good at a race?" "No," said he, "but my big bull dog is, and he has been trained to assist me in my office these several years; he will take any man down at my bidding." "Well, Mr. Peabody, you compelled me to go a mile, I have gone with you two miles. You have given me an opportunity to preach, sing, and have also entertained me with lodging and breakfast. I must now go on my journey; if you are good at a race you can accompany me. I thank you for all your kindness—good day, sir."

I then started on my journey, while he stood amazed and not able to step one foot before the other. Seeing this, I halted, turned to him and again invited him to a race. He still stood amazed. I then renewed my exertions, and soon increased my speed to something like that of a deer. He did not awake from his astonishment sufficiently to start in pursuit till I had gained, perhaps, two hundred yards. I had already leaped a fence, and was making my way through a field to the forest on the right of the road. He now came hallooing after me, and shouting to his dog to seize me. The dog, being one of the largest I ever saw, came close on my footsteps with all his fury; the officer behind still in pursuit, clapping his hands and hallooing, "stu-boy, stu-boy—take him—watch—lay hold of him, I say—down with him," and pointing his finger in the direction I was running. The dog was fast overtaking me, and in the act of leaping upon me, when, quick as lightning, the thought struck me, to assist the officer, in sending the dog with all fury to the forest a little distance before me. I pointed my finger in that direction, clapped my hands, and shouted in imitation of the officer. The dog hastened past me with redoubled speed towards the forest; being urged by the officer and myself, and both of us running in the same direction.

Gaining the forest, I soon lost sight of the officer and dog, and have not seen them since (*Autobiography*, 36–39).

* * *

While he was serving as president of the British Mission, Hugh B. Brown met with an ex-army officer, a diplomatic correspondent, who had been assigned to write a series of articles opposing the Church.

"I thought it only fair," the man explained, "to come to you and talk about it before starting those articles."

President Brown asked, "You say you are going to write against the Church?"

"I certainly am," the man said. "What I am going to write will not be good, will not be favorable."

"It is interesting that you know enough about the Mormons to write authoritatively about them," commented President Brown. When the man admitted he knew nothing, President Brown hospitably invited him to spend thirty days in the mission home's library. . . . "I thought it only fair to warn him that if he spent thirty days in that library reading on Mormonism, he would ask for baptism," wrote President Brown later.

"Why, the idea that I would become a Mormon is preposterous!" the writer answered.

The man studied in the mission home library. Meanwhile, Hugh B. Brown was released as mission president and returned home to Utah. Less than thirty days after his interview with the anti-Mormon writer, Brother Brown received a cable from the man: "I think you will be interested to know that I am being baptized next Friday" (see Brown, *An Abundant Life,* ed. Firmage, 107–8).

* * *

In 1915, Willard Bean and his new bride, Rebecca, were called by President Joseph F. Smith to serve a mission of at least five years in Palmyra, New York. The mission lasted, as it turned out, nearly twenty-five years. Initially, Brother Bean and his family were not well received by the townspeople of Palmyra, who were antagonistic toward the Church. One day Willard, a former boxing champion, was challenged by a man who was watering his garden. The man suddenly turned his garden hose on Willard and taunted, "I understand you believe in baptism by immersion." Brother Bean vaulted over the fence separating them, took a fighting stance, and replied, "Yes, and we also believe in the laying on of hands!" (see *The Fighting Parson,* quoted in *Ensign,* May 1994, 48).

Mistakes

Hugh B. Brown: We shall begin these services by the chorus singing a Latter-day hymn medley, with Jay Powells as socialist. . . . I hope Brother Powells will not start an action for slander (Conference Report, Apr. 1966, 91).

* * *

Robert L. Simpson: Speaking of getting off to a bad start, I think I hold the record. As I was watching the Rose Bowl game on television the other day, I had a flashback of something that happened to me many years ago on a high school football field, not too far from that Rose Bowl.

It was my first year of high school football. I'd been playing second string all through the practice games, and this was the first big league game. Six thousand cheering people were in the stands. As we were breaking our halftime pep talk, the coach suddenly said, "Simpson, you start the second half."

The old adrenaline came rushing, and I went charging out onto the field. This was my chance! Just about that time the coach suddenly said, "Oh, and by the way, I want you to kick off, Simpson."

I determined right then and there that I was going to kick that ball farther than any football had ever been kicked in history. I really wanted to make a good showing on my first chance on the first string. Well, the referee waved his arm and blew his whistle. I could hear those six thousand people. I looked at the ball and came charging down the field. I felt everything tingling in my body—the excitement was so high!

Well, you have probably already guessed it, I missed the ball. Six thousand people went wild. But that isn't the half of it. This was back in the days when the quarterback held the ball with his finger. I broke the quarterback's finger.

Now, if you think that you're off to a bad start, I just want to set your mind at ease and let you know that it could be worse. I also want you to know that I had a coach that had confidence in me . . . because he left me in. I don't know why, but he did . . . and I played the rest of the game. If I weren't so modest, I might also tell you that I made all-league that year (*Speeches of the Year,* 1975, 319–20).

MONEY

*   J O K E S   *

At one time John was true and faithful in the Church. But he became so consumed with making money that he began to work seven days a week and became inactive.

"John," a friend protested, "you shouldn't think about money all the time. You can't take it with you, you know."

"Is that so?" John answered. "Then I will not go."

* * *

Client: Well, now that you've examined my records, how am I doing financially?

Accountant: Well, sir, I can give you the same odds the Lord gave Noah.

Client: What would that be?

Accountant: You've got forty days and forty nights to keep from going under.

* * *

Husband: Hi, dear! I've got good news and more good news!

Wife: What is it?

Husband: First—we don't have to move to a more expensive apartment after all! And second—guess why? Our landlord has raised our rent.

* * *

They say the auto industry employs more than a million workers. How can so many people make a living from something nobody has paid for?

* * *

Joanne: Here it is the middle of February, and we're still cleaning up from Christmas.

Tammy: What? Still cleaning up?

Joanne: Yes. First we cleaned out our checking account. Then we cleaned out our savings account. Now we're going through drawers looking for spare change.

* * *

Our family went shopping for a larger family car last week. A salesman came over and said, "Take a look! They're bigger than ever and they last a lifetime." Unfortunately he was talking about the payments, not the cars.

* * *

Living within a budget saves money because by the time you've balanced it, it's too late to go anywhere.

* * *

I believe in living within my income—even if I have to borrow money to do it.

* * *

It's really hard to save money when your neighbors keep buying things you can't afford.

* * *

Misers aren't fun to live with, but they sure do make terrific ancestors.

* * *

A farmer who had just planted a large field of corn commented to his neighbor, "I sure hope I break even this year. I really need the money."

* * *

Two men stood before the casket of a wealthy friend. "How much property did he leave?" asked one.

"All of it," replied the other.

* **P O E M S** *

Joseph Fielding Smith: Asael [Smith, grandfather of Joseph Smith] was gifted with the pen and did considerable writing in his day. He was affable in manner, possessing a quaint and genial humor and a fund of anecdotes. While living in Topsfield he expressed to the selectmen of that town the amount and nature of his taxable property in this manner:—

> I have two poles tho' one is poor,
> I have three cown & want five more,
> I have not horse, But fifteen sheep;
> No more than these this year I keep,
> Stears, that's two years old, one pair,
> Two calves I have, all over hair,
> Three heffers two years old, I own
> One heffer calf that's poorly grone,
> My land is acres Eighty two
> Which search the Record youle find true,
> And this is all I have in store,
> I'll thank you if youle Tax no more.

(*Life of Joseph F. Smith*, 21).

*   Q U O T A T I O N S   *

John Taylor: You have had hard times; still you are living and thriving: there are none of you naked or without shoes, hats or bonnets. You seem to be provided with a great many of the good things of this life. You seem to be doing tolerably well. I know very well that you have a hard struggle to make two ends meet; I understand it. But there is one advantage you have—no one will want to steal away your place from you; will they? (Laughter.) I do not think they would want to carry it off. I do not think they would want to drive you away because of your extraneous wealth; consequently, you are free from this trouble (*Journal of Discourses* 23:16).

*   *   *

N. Eldon Tanner: After our youngest daughter had started school, she came home just before Christmas and said to her mother, "Do you know what they say about Santa Claus in school?"

Her mother said, "No, what do they say?"

She replied, "They say there is no Santa Claus and it's our parents who give us Christmas gifts."

Her mother asked, "And what did you say?"

"I told them, 'You don't know my daddy and mother!'"

* * *

Milton R. Hunter: What is there in all the world that you would rather have than anything else? What is the goal for which you would seek? When I had asked my college students those two questions, several of them would immediately raise their hands. Some of the big boys on the back row would snap their fingers and be quite excited, thinking they had the right answer, and so I would call on them. They always answered the same way. They said, "A million dollars" or "A Cadillac."

I spent a few minutes trying to convince them that a million dollars was not the most vital thing in the world. In fact, I even endeavored to convince them that it might even be detrimental to a person to have that much money. At least I convinced myself that I had convinced them to that effect.

You know, I have never read in the scriptures where Jesus said, "For, behold, a million dollars is the greatest gift of God." I observe by your smiles and laughter that you haven't either. Nor have I read wherein the Savior said, "He who hath a million dollars is rich indeed." It does not sound like scripture (*Speeches of the Year,* 12 May 1964, 2).

* * *

J. Golden Kimball: My father [Heber C. Kimball] died in 1868. When his administrators divided up the estate there was not a single silver dollar given to any of his children, to my knowledge, but there was some property. Our father selected land on the side hill, among the rocks—he wanted to get away from the center of the city. He owned what is known as the Capitol Hill. He left his children that real estate. There was one lot that was given to my mother's family, and I owned one third of it. I received twenty-five thousand dollars for my portion, and I have been very sorry twenty-five thousand times that I ever sold it. . . . I am thankful we had sense enough to keep sufficient ground to bury our posterity on. We have paid taxes on it ever since I was fifteen years old, and I still hold it. What about the other property? There is now hardly a Kimball to be found on the Capitol Hill—unless it be those that are dead (Conference Report, Oct. 1909, 111).

* * *

J. Golden Kimball: I am in sympathy with the people. I know we have all been foolish. I am foolish. I don't think there is a bigger fool than an old fool. A man who has had experience ought to know better. One of my brethren said to me and he is a man so kind and gentle that I had every reason to believe he would extend to me a little sympathy—I told him of one of my last speculations and he said: "If you are as big a sucker as that you ought to take your medicine." I said: "I am taking it, and it is not sugar-coated either." (Laughter)

I met a banker a few weeks ago—we were very friendly. Thank the Lord, I do not owe that bank anything, but I owe another bank. (Laughter) I said: "How are things going?"

"Well, we are taking everything but their suspenders."

I thought afterwards that I should have said to him: If that bank hasn't got any more elasticity than my suspenders, I will throw them in (Conference Report, Oct. 1931, 57).

* STORIES *

N. Eldon Tanner told the story of an immigrant father who ran his business very simply, keeping his accounts payable in a shoe box, his accounts receivable on a spindle, and his cash in the cash register.

"I don't see how you can run your business this way," said the man's son. "How do you know what your profit is?"

"Son," answered the businessman, "when I got off the boat, I had only the pants I was wearing. Today your sister is an art teacher, your brother is a doctor, and you're an accountant. I have a car, a home, and a good business. Everything is paid for. So you add it all up, subtract the pants, and there's my profit" (Durham, *N. Eldon Tanner,* 286).

* * *

After John C. Bennett became estranged from the Church, he decided he wanted to come back to Nauvoo. Joseph Smith extended a warm welcome, but he held out no material inducements or false hopes—only the possibility of spiritual blessings. He concluded an August 1840 letter to Bennett in this way: "My general invitation is, Let all that will, come, and partake of the poverty of Nauvoo freely" (Regional Studies, Illinois, Skinner—John C. Bennett, 252–53).

* * *

Spencer W. Kimball once decided against taking an option on some property on the Las Vegas "Strip." He didn't want ties to gambling, but he also didn't know the full value of the option until later. He said of the incident, "It is good we didn't buy that property. We'd unavoidably have been multimillionaires, and I don't think I could have stood it" (Kimball, "Spencer W. Kimball," *BYU Studies* 25[4]: 64).

MORMONISM

* J O K E S *

A man from New York visited his Mormon friend in Salt Lake City one summer. They went together to the mall—and the Mormon left his car unlocked. Then they went to the grocery store—and the Mormon left his car unlocked. Then they drove home—and the Mormon left the keys in his car. The next day they went to church together—and the Mormon removed the keys and locked the door before entering the meeting.

"I don't get it," the friend exclaimed. "Here you don't lock your car at the mall or the grocery store—you even leave the keys in the ignition all night at your home. But when you go to church you lock your car. Why?"

"Simple," the man said. "If I don't lock it here, when I come back out it will be filled with zucchini."

* * *

A Primary teacher was so stressed and frustrated that she decided she needed to seek medical help. "I'm feeling more stress than I ever have in my life," she told her doctor.

"What do you think might be causing it?"

"Well, I'm pretty sure it's the Sunbeams."

The doctor began to write on his pad. "Oh, yes? The sunbeams?"

"They're always talking," the woman said. "I can't get them to be quiet."

"I see," said the doctor. "And what do they say?"

"Well, what they say isn't all that important. It's just that they're so noisy! And when I want to talk to them they won't listen."

"I've never heard of such a thing," the doctor said, still taking notes.

"Well, it's just terrible . . ." the woman paused and looked at the doctor. "Wait a minute! You're not LDS are you?"

MOTHERHOOD

* J O K E S *

A mother with four children in tow boarded a bus. They gave the driver so much trouble that he said at the end of the trip, "Lady, you ought to leave half your kids at home."

The woman looked at him, sighed, and said, "I did."

* * *

Mom: Eat your spinach, Kimberly. It will put color in your cheeks.
Kimberly: But, Mom, who wants green cheeks?

* * *

Teenager: Did you make a New Year's resolution this year, Mom?
Mom: Yes. I'm going to stop correcting you children all the time.
Teenager: Wow! Well, believe me, nobody will appreciate that more than me.
Mom: More than *I*.

* * *

Miss Jones was giving her second-grade students a lesson on science. "Here is a magnet," she said. "It's made of a kind of metal. Look how it can pick up nails, bobby pins, and other bits of iron." The class watched, fascinated.

Then, by way of review, she said, "All right, class. My name begins with the letter 'M' and I pick up things. What am I?"

A little boy on the front row said, "You're a mother."

* S T O R I E S *

John Sonnenberg, a former member of the Second Quorum of the Seventy, tells this story about his young family: At the time he was beginning his practice as a dentist, the Sonnenbergs had seven young children and just one car. When his wife wanted to go anywhere, she and the children took the bus.

One day as she and the seven kids all boarded a bus, the driver, amazed, asked, "Lady, are these all your children, or is this a picnic?"

"They are all my children," she answered, "and believe me, it's no picnic!" (*Ensign*, Nov. 1983, 36).

MOTIVATION

* J O K E S *

One day a small frog fell in a large rut that a passing wagon wheel had made in the muddy road. He tried and tried to get out but was not making much progress.

Another frog heard his cries and came to help him. But to his amazement, when he arrived, his friend had already pulled himself out.

"How did you do it?" asked the friend.

"I had to," replied the frog. "A wagon was coming."

MUSIC

* J O K E S *

An LDS vocalist decided to sing "Come, Come Ye Saints" as her entry in a national talent contest. During her somewhat overblown performance, she noticed a man in the audience who was weeping profusely. After the competition, she sought him out. "Pardon me," she asked. "Are you LDS?" "No," he replied, shaking his head. "I'm a musician."

* * *

A young boy was practicing the violin, and the family dog joined in with repeated loud howling. Finally the father couldn't stand the racket any longer. "Son," he hollered above the din. "Couldn't you play a tune the dog doesn't know?"

* Q U O T A T I O N S *

Spencer W. Kimball: I am comforted with the assurance that there will be beautiful music in heaven, for which I am most grateful. Some say there will be no music in that other place—but then some sounds that are passed off as music seem to belong in that other place (*Church News*, 2 Oct. 1982, 3).

* * *

Hugh B. Brown: I think nothing finer can be or has been given than these numbers tonight by this chorus. Of course, I don't profess to be much of a judge of music. I fear I may be a little like a couple of fellows who were sitting in a bandstand where a band was playing.

167

Each wanted to impress the other with his knowledge of music. One said, "Do you know what the band's playing?"

"Why, yes! That's Tannhauser!"

"No, it's the second movement of Chopin."

The other said "I'll go down and find out." He went down toward the bandstand, came back shortly, and said, "We're both wrong. That was the 'Refrain from Spitting.' I saw it on the sign out there" (Brown, "Father, Are You There?" 1959, audio tape).

* * *

Heber J. Grant: Upon my recent trip to Arizona, I asked Elders Rudger Clawson and J. Golden Kimball if they had any objections to my singing one hundred hymns that day. They took it as a joke, and assured me that they would be delighted. We were on the way from Holbrook to St. Johns, a distance of about sixty miles. After I had sung about forty times, they assured me that if I sang the remaining sixty they would be sure to have nervous prostration. I paid no attention whatever to their appeal, but held them to their bargain and sang the full one hundred. One hundred and fifteen songs in one day and four hundred in four days, is the largest amount of practicing I ever did (*Improvement Era* 3:886–90).

* * *

George Albert Smith: The music, as we have already been informed, for this session of the Conference, is by the Manti Choir, 120 voices strong. The hymns that are to be rendered by this choir have been sung by this organization for upwards of sixty years. Among them are the compositions and arrangements of Professor A. C. Smyth, the first leader of the choir. I remember Brother Smyth very well. He is one of the men who tried to teach me how to sing (Conference Report, Apr. 1946, 55).

* * *

Heber J. Grant: I am perfectly willing to go along as slowly as the Lord wants, but the quicker I get so that I can talk faster and get more accustomed to these false teeth, the better I will like it. . . .

I am free to confess that I do not like the sound of my own voice worth a cent. . . .

I am very sorry, after laboring more diligently, I believe, than anybody else ever did to try to learn to sing a song, that I cannot sing any more. But I have been practicing bass sitting next to Brother McKay here today, and I have concluded that I had better join the bass choir, . . . and say goodbye to the lead (Conference Report, Apr. 1941, 128).

* * *

President Ulysses S. Grant had a heartfelt dislike for all music. Once at a concert in Baltimore, his companion asked him if he recognized a particular piece. "Actually," Grant said, "I know only two tunes. One is 'Yankee Doodle' and the other isn't."

* STORIES *

When President Joseph Fielding Smith and his wife Jessie visited wards or stakes, they often ended up singing musical duets together. Jessie, a former member of the Tabernacle Choir, had a beautiful singing voice and accompanied them on the piano. President Smith often turned to the congregation and said, "She calls this a duet; I call it a Do-It. I have to do it whether I want to or not." At the conclusion of the musical number, President Smith would say to the congregation, "I appreciate that you folks didn't walk out on me."

Once as they were driving back to Salt Lake City after an impromptu musical number had been performed at a BYU devotional, President Smith's secretary, Arthur Haycock, turned to him and said, "President Smith, those people loved you, and they enjoyed your singing. Did you see they were weeping during your duet?"

President Smith quickly responded, "I can understand that. My singing is enough to make anybody cry" (Swinton, *In the Company of Prophets*, 62).

NEIGHBORLINESS

* JOKES *

Brother Bernstein was thoroughly annoyed when his neighbor called at two o'clock in the morning and said, "Your stupid dog is barking so loud I can't sleep!" The neighbor slammed the phone down without even waiting for an answer.

The following night Brother Bernstein waited until 2:00 A.M., then called his neighbor back and said, "I don't have a dog."

OBEDIENCE

* JOKES *

Too many people treat the Ten Commandments as if they were part of a university exam: "Choose eight of the following ten . . ."

* S T O R I E S *

An unprincipled businessman, who liked to appear full of virtue, told Mark Twain, "Before I die, I'm going to make a pilgrimage to the Holy Land. I shall climb to the top of Mount Sinai and read the Ten Commandments aloud."

"I have a better idea," said Mark Twain.

"You do?"

"Why don't you stay home in Boston and *keep* them."

* * *

Henry Ward Beecher was once contemplating buying a horse. The famous preacher was shown many horses by the owner of the stables. The owner, however, had particularly high praise for a certain, fine-looking animal.

"Now here's a horse that's really sound. He can go any gait. He stands without hitching; works any place you put him; goes when you want him to and stops the minute you say 'Whoa.' He is perfectly gentle, yet full of spirits. He has no bad traits, doesn't kick, doesn't bite. Comes when you call him and doesn't run off when he sees something strange."

With a wistful look in his eye, Mr. Beecher sighed, "If only that horse were a member of my church."

OPINION

* QUOTATIONS *

Heber J. Grant: I am a thorough convert myself to the idea that it is not possible for all men to see alike. You know the remark made by a man once: "It is a splendid thing that we do not all see alike, because if we did, everybody would want to marry my Sally Ann" (Conference Report, Oct. 1919, 19).

ORDER

* QUOTATIONS *

Jedediah M. Grant on keeping a house of order: Some here keep their children too dirty for admission into a district school where I was raised; and in some houses the towels look as though they had passed Noah's ark, or had been used by some of the inhabitants of Sodom and Gomorrah, and the knives and forks have the appearance of having been rusting ever since Adam was driven from the Garden of Eden (*Journal of Discourses* 4:73).

* STORIES *

When Spencer W. Kimball was president of the Church, the First Presidency and Quorum of the Twelve often had lunch together after their weekly meeting in the Salt Lake Temple. After lunch, they usually passed around a box of chocolates, beginning with the First Presidency. By the time the box got down to the newest member of the Twelve, however, the light chocolates had always been taken. At one meeting, the junior member said, "Is there any chance to reverse the usual order of choosing chocolates? I don't care for dark chocolate and that is all there is left by the time the box gets to me."

President Kimball replied, "If you live long enough, you'll move up into the light chocolates" (Kimball, "Spencer W. Kimball," *BYU Studies* 25[4]: 65).

PARENTHOOD

* J O K E S *

College student to parents: "Dear Mom and Dad: Don't forget to write, even if it's only ten or twenty."

* * *

On his first visit to the zoo, a little boy stared at the caged stork for a long while. Then he turned to his father and exclaimed, "Gee, Dad, he doesn't recognize me!"

* * *

The problem with being a parent is that by the time you've learned how to do your job, you're unemployed.

* * *

How Parents Mature

When you're 4 years old: My parents can do anything.

When you're 7 years old: My parents know a whole lot.

When you're 9: My parents don't know quite everything.

When you're 12: Parents just don't understand.

When you're 14: Parents are old-fashioned.

When you're 19: My parents are out of touch.

When you're 25: Parents are okay.

When you're 30: I wonder what my parents think about this?

When you're 35: I must get my parents' input first.

When you're 50: What would my parents have thought about that?

When you're 60: I wish I could talk it over with my parents once more.

* * *

The mother of a teenaged boy was talking to a ward member whose son was always well-groomed and tidy. "My son just leaves his shirt hanging out all the time," the first woman complained. "How do you get your son to tuck his in?"

"It's easy," answered her friend. "I just sew lace onto the bottom of all his shirts."

* * *

You know you're an experienced parent if . . .

You count the sprinkles on each kid's cupcake to make sure they're equal.

You hide in the bathroom just to get some private time.

You consider fingerpaint to be a controlled substance.

You've mastered the fine art of placing huge quantities of scrambled eggs and pancakes on the same plate without anything "touching."

You hope ketchup is a vegetable because it's the only one your child eats.

You con your kid into thinking that "Toys R Us" is a toy *museum* and not really a store.

You fast-forward through the scene where Bambi's mom gets killed.

You hire a sitter because you and your spouse haven't been out in ages, then spend half the night calling home to check on the kids.

You start offering to cut up other people's food for them!

* * *

A mother was worried because her teenage daughter had been calling a certain boy too often. So she posted a sign over the telephone: "Is this call necessary?"

The next day another sign appeared, directly below the first: "How do I know until I've made the call?"

* * *

A young father carried his screaming baby out of sacrament meeting and into the foyer. "There, there," he said. "Take it easy. Control yourself. Calm down."

The baby immediately became quiet.

Another father in the foyer said, "Boy, you sure know how to talk to a baby."

"Baby!" the first father said. "I was talking to myself!"

* Q U O T A T I O N S *

Brigham Young: Through imbibing false ideas, principles and teachings, children become as the old [man] said. The missionary had been trying to instruct him in the saying, "Bring up a child in the way he should go, and when he is old he will not depart from it;" the old [man] gave it a little different interpretation. Said he, "Bring up a child and away he goes." So it is now—we bring up children and away they go (*Journal of Discourses* 13:251–52).

* * *

David O. McKay: After a lecture by the late Francis Wayland Parker, a great Chicago educator, a woman asked:
"How early can I begin the education of my child?"
"When will your child be born?" asked the educator.
"Born?" she gasped. "Why, he is already five years old."
"My goodness, woman," he cried, "don't stand here talking to me—hurry home; already you have lost the best five years" (*Relief Society Magazine*, Dec. 1953, 792).

* * *

N. Eldon Tanner: We have five daughters. Four of them were courting at one time, or being courted. I do not know which it was. One of those girls had a girl friend in the house this evening and two young men called for them. I sat and talked to them. . . . and just before they were ready to leave, I said, "Now, have a good time." Then just as they were going out of the door I went over to my daughter and I said, "Now, behave yourself."
She said, "Well, Dad, make up your mind" (*Speeches of the Year,* 27 Mar. 1963, 9).

* STORIES *

Lord Rochester, John Wilmot (1647–1680), said to a group, "When I was young, I had six theories on how to bring up children."
"And, pray, what are your theories?" asked someone.
"There is no use in asking," replied Rochester. "Now I have six children and no theories."

PATIENCE

* J O K E S *

A man entered a restaurant on the banks of the Chesapeake Bay, sat down, and looked rather impatient and grouchy. At last a waiter appeared.

"It's about time!" said the man. "Now tell me. Do you serve crabs here?"

"Certainly, sir," replied the waiter, "we serve anyone."

PEACE

* J O K E S *

An old man who had had more than his share of challenges was asked how he managed to stay so cheerful. "Well, I'll tell you," he replied. "I've just learned to cooperate with the inevitable."

* S T O R I E S *

Shortly before the death of Thoreau, a pious aunt visited him and asked, "Have you made your peace with God, Henry?"

"I don't know that we ever quarreled," he replied.

177

PERFECTION

* J O K E S *

When you aim for perfection, you find that it's a moving target.

* * *

To illustrate his point to the congregation, the high councilor asked for anyone who was perfect to stand up. To his surprise, a man in the back of the chapel rose to his feet. "You mean to say you're actually perfect?" the high councilor asked.

"Well, no," the man replied. "I'm acting as proxy for my wife's first husband."

* * *

Teacher: How much is four times four, Kenny?
Kenny: Sixteen.
Teacher: That's pretty good.
Kenny: Pretty good? I'd call it perfect.

PERSECUTION

* Q U O T A T I O N S *

George Albert Smith: In the history of our persecutions there have arisen a great many anecdotes; but one will perhaps serve to illustrate the condition in which I wish to see every man that raises in these mountains the hand of oppression upon the innocent. I wish to see such men rigged out with the same honors and comforts as was the honorable Samuel C. Owen, Commander-in-Chief of the Jackson County mob. He, with eleven men, was engaged at a mass meeting, to raise a mob to drive the Saints from Clay County. This was in the year 1834, in the month of June. They had made speeches, and done everything to raise the indignation of the people against the Saints. In the evening, himself, James Campbell, and nine others, commenced to cross the Missouri river on their way home again; and the Lord, or some accident, knocked a hole in the bottom of the boat. When they discovered it, says Commander Owen to the company on the ferry boat, "We must strip to the bone, or we shall all perish." Mr. Campbell replied, "I will go to hell before I will land naked." He had his choice, and went to the bottom. Owen stripped himself of every article of clothing, and commenced floating down the river. After making several attempts he finally landed on the Jackson side of the river, after a swim of about fourteen miles. He rested some time, being perfectly exhausted, and then started into the nettles, which grow very thick and to a great height, in the Missouri bottoms, and which was his only possible chance in making from the river to the settlements. He had to walk four miles through the nettles, which took him the remainder of the night, and when he got through the nettles, he came to a road, and saw a young lady approaching on horseback, who was the belle of Jackson County. In this miserable condition he laid himself behind a log, so that she could not see him. When she arrived opposite the log, he says, "Madam, I am Samuel C. Owen, the Commander-in-Chief of the mob against the Mormons; I wish you to send some men from the next house with clothing, for I am naked." The lady in her philanthropy dismounted, and left him a light shawl and a certain unmentionable under garment, and passed on. So His Excellency Samuel C. Owen, who was afterwards killed in Mexico by foolishly exposing himself, contrary to orders, took up his line of march for the town, in the shawl and petticoat uniform, after his expedition against the "Mormons."

My young friends, have the goodness to use every man so, who comes into your country to mob and oppress the innocent; and LADIES, DON'T LEND HIM ANY CLOTHING (*Journal of Discourses* 2:24).

* * *

David O. McKay in general conference: I have a note here that there are [anti-Mormon] literature distributors at our gates [on temple square]. We implore those who receive the leaflets that are being passed out not to throw them on the street. Please cooperate with our City Fathers and use the receptacles that have been furnished by our city officials (Conference Report, Oct. 1956, 18).

* * *

Brigham Young: Ask yourselves whether you think this people would have received as much as they have received, if they never had been persecuted. Could they have advanced in the school of intelligence as far without being persecuted, as they have by being persecuted? Look for instance at Adam. Listen, ye Latter-day Saints! Supposing that Adam was formed actually out of clay, out of the same kind of material from which bricks are formed; that with this matter God made the pattern of a man, and breathed into it the breath of life, and left it there, in that state of supposed perfection, he would have been an adobie to this day. He would not have known anything (*Journal of Discourses* 2:6).

* * *

George A. Smith: Every person who is well acquainted with the history of this Church knows that at the commencement of it the persecutions commenced, and they continued to increase until the death of the Prophet. Forty-seven times he was arraigned before the tribunals of law, and had to sustain all the expense of defending himself in those vexatious suits, and was every time acquitted. He was never found guilty but once. I have been told, by Patriarch Emer Harris, that on a certain occasion he was brought before a magistrate in the State of New York, and charged with having cast out devils; the magistrate, after hearing the witnesses, decided that he was guilty, but as the statutes of New York did not provide a punishment for casting out devils, he was acquitted (*Journal of Discourses* 2:213).

* * *

Brigham Young: Joseph Smith was arraigned before Judge Austin A. King, on a charge of treason. The Judge inquired of Mr. Smith, "Do you believe and teach the doctrine that in the course of time the Saints will possess the earth?" Joseph replied that he did. "Do you believe that the Lord will raise up a kingdom that will fill the whole earth and rule over all other kingdoms, as the Prophet Daniel has said?" "Yes, sir, I believe that Jesus Christ will reign king of nations as he does king of Saints." "Write that down, clerk; we want to fasten upon him the charge of treason, for if he believes this, he must believe that the State of Missouri will crumble and fall to rise no more." Lawyer Doniphan said to the Judge, " . . . Judge, you had better make the Bible treason and have done with it" (*Journal of Discourses* 9:331).

* * *

Heber C. Kimball: Suppose the Gentiles were to try to put it down, and to kill brother Brigham, and me, and brother Daniel, and the Twelve Apostles, still there are some fifty or sixty Quorums of Seventies that are capable of spreading abroad this kingdom. Why, bless you, it is like the mustard seed: you know it is most troublesome to get out of the garden. You get vexed with it and go and kick it about, and by that means you make ten thousand more little mustard trees.

Well, you know they drove us far away into these mountains; and now see the multitude of little mustard trees that are growing up! (*Journal of Discourses* 5:8).

* * *

Orson F. Whitney: Orson Pratt was as high-spirited as he was fearless and determined. He was preaching, at Liverpool, in the open air, when a noisy fellow, pushing his way through the crowd and planting himself squarely in front, began to denounce him. The speaker, without deigning to notice the interruption, raised his stentorian voice, and going right on with his discourse, poured forth a volume of sound that completely drowned the voice of his would-be disturber. The fellow then shouted his objections, but the Apostle, still further increasing his own lung power, again rendered the tones of the hoodlum inaudible. This was kept up until the latter ceased from sheer exhaustion, and retired amid the laughter of the bystanders (Conference Report, Oct. 1911, 68).

* **S T O R I E S** *

Brigham Young: I do not profess to be much of a joker, but I do think this to be one of the best jokes ever perpetrated.

By the time we were at work in the Nauvoo Temple, officiating in the ordinances, the mob had learned that "Mormonism" was not dead, as they had supposed. We had completed the walls of the Temple, and the attic story from about half way up of the first windows, in about fifteen months. It went up like magic, and we commenced officiating in the ordinances. Then the mob commenced to hunt for other victims; they had already killed the Prophets Joseph and Hyrum in Carthage jail, while under the pledge of the State for their safety, and now they wanted Brigham, the President of the Twelve Apostles, who were then acting as the Presidency of the Church.

I was in my room in the Temple; it was in the south-east corner of the upper story. I learned that a posse was lurking around the Temple, and that the United States Marshal was waiting for me to come down, whereupon I knelt down and asked my Father in heaven, in the name of Jesus, to guide and protect me that I might live to prove advantageous to the Saints. Just as I arose from my knees and sat down in my chair, there came a rap at my door. I said, "Come in," and Brother George D. Grant, who was then engaged driving my carriage and doing chores for me, entered the room.

Said he, "Brother Young, do you know that a posse and the United States Marshal are here?" I told him I had heard so. On entering the room Brother Grant left the door open. Nothing came into my mind what to do, until looking directly across the hall I saw Brother William Miller leaning against the wall.

As I stepped towards the door I beckoned to him; he came. Said I to him, "Brother William, the Marshal is here for me; will you go and do just as I tell you? If you will, I will serve them a trick." I knew that Brother Miller was an excellent man, perfectly reliable and capable of carrying out my project. Said I, "Here, take my cloak;" but it happened to be Brother Heber C. Kimball's; our cloaks were alike in color, fashion and size. I threw it around his shoulders, and told him to wear my hat and accompany Brother George D. Grant. He did so. I said to Brother Grant, "George, you step into the carriage and look towards Brother Miller, and say to him, as though you were addressing me, 'Are you ready to ride?' You can do this, and they will suppose Brother Miller to be me, and proceed accordingly," which they did.

Just as Brother Miller was entering the carriage, the Marshal stepped up to him, and, placing his hand upon his shoulder, said, "You are my prisoner." Brother William entered the carriage and said to the Marshal, "I am going to the Mansion House, won't you ride with me?" They both went to the Mansion House. There were my sons Joseph A., Brigham, Jr., and Brother Heber C. Kimball's boys, and others who were looking on, and all seemed at once to understand and partake of the joke. They followed the carriage to the Mansion House and gathered around Brother Miller, with tears in their eyes, saying, "Father, or President Young, where are you going?" Brother

Miller looked at them kindly, but made no reply; and the Marshal really thought he had got "Brother Brigham."

Lawyer Edmonds, who was then staying at the Mansion House, appreciating the joke, volunteered to Brother Miller to go to Carthage with him and see him safe through. When they arrived within two or three miles of Carthage, the Marshal with his posse stopped. They arose in their carriages, buggies and waggons, and, like a tribe of Indians going into battle, or as if they were a pack of demons, yelling and shouting, they exclaimed, "We've got him! We've got him! We've got him!"

When they reached Carthage the Marshal took the supposed Brigham into an upper room of the hotel, and placed a guard over him, at the same time telling those around that he had got him. Brother Miller remained in the room until they bid him come to supper. While there, parties came in, one after the other, and asked for Brigham. Brother Miller was pointed out to them. So it continued, until an apostate Mormon, by the name of Thatcher, who had lived in Nauvoo, came in, sat down and asked the landlord where Brigham Young was. The landlord, pointing across the table to Brother Miller, said, "That is Mr. Young." Thatcher replied, "Where? I can't see any one that looks like Brigham." The landlord told him it was that fat, fleshy man eating. "Oh, h___!" exclaimed Thatcher, "that's not Brigham; that is William Miller, one of my old neighbors."

Upon hearing this the landlord went, and, tapping the Sheriff on the shoulder, took him a few steps to one side, and said, "You have made a mistake, that is not Brigham Young; it is William Miller, of Nauvoo." The Marshal, very much astonished, exclaimed, "Good heavens! and he passed for Brigham." He then took Brother Miller into a room, and, turning to him, said, "What in h___ is the reason you did not tell me your name?"

Brother Miller replied, "You have not asked me my name."

"Well," said the Sheriff, with another oath, "What is your name?"

"My name," he replied, "is William Miller."

Said the Marshal, "I thought your name was Brigham Young. Do you say this for a fact?"

"Certainly I do," said Brother Miller.

"Then," said the Marshal, "why did you not tell me this before?"

"I was under no obligations to tell you," replied Brother Miller, "as you did not ask me."

Then the Marshal, in a rage, walked out of the room, followed by Brother Miller, who walked off in company with Lawyer Edmonds, Sheriff Backenstos, and others, who took him across lots to a place of safety; and this is the real pith of the story of "Bogus" Brigham, as far as I can recollect (*Journal of Discourses* 14:218–19).

PERSEVERANCE

* JOKES *

"You may well feel proud of yourself, young fellow," said a busy executive to a life insurance agent. "I've refused to see seven insurance men today."

"I know," said the agent, "I'm them."

* QUOTATIONS *

Heber C. Kimball: I stick to "Mormonism," and I pray God that it may stick to me (*Journal of Discourses* 3:231).

* * *

Brigham Young: I recollect many times when Brother Joseph, reflecting upon how many would come into the Kingdom of God and go out again, would say, "Brethren, I have not apostatized yet, and don't feel like doing so" (*Journal of Discourses* 2:257).

* * *

Orson F. Whitney: Our grandfathers and grandmothers, our parents, who came from Scandinavia, from Germany, from Switzerland, from England, Scotland, and Wales, from Australia and the islands of the sea, from Canada and the States of the Union, braving every hardship, facing every peril, laying their all upon the altar, coming out and fighting for God and His divine purpose—they are called by some "the offscourings of the earth," "the scum of creation!" Perhaps it is because they "came out on top!" (Conference Report, Apr. 1915, 101).

* * *

Heber J. Grant: I have, all the days of my life, enjoyed singing very much. When I was a little boy ten years of age I joined a singing class, and the professor told me that I could never learn to sing. Some years ago I had my character read by a phrenologist and he told me that I could sing, but he said he would like to be forty miles away while I was doing it. . . . I was practicing singing a few weeks ago in the Templeton building, and the room where I was doing so was next to that of a dentist. The people in the hall decided that someone was having his teeth extracted. . . . All the days of my life I have tried to sing "O My Father," written by Sister Eliza R. Snow. . . . I remarked some four months ago to Brother Horace S. Ensign that I would be willing to spend four or five months of my spare time if I could only learn to sing that one hymn. He told me that any one could learn to sing that had perseverance. I said to him if there was anything that I had it was perseverance. So I suggested that we sit down and I would take my first lesson of two hours on that song. I have been continuing the lessons on it ever since. . . . I have sung it as high as 115 times in one day. I have practiced on the "Doxology" between three and four hundred times, and there are only four lines, and I cannot sing it yet. . . . I traveled from Holbrook, Arizona, to St. John, with Brothers Clawson and Kimball, some months ago, and I sang one hundred times that day and gave them nervous prostration. . . . Now I tried to sing "O My Father" at Snowflake, Arizona, and I only got as far as the "O," and I did not get that right. . . . After five or six weeks of hard study, and after singing one hymn thousands of times, to sing a little I decided not to read these songs to the children, but to learn to sing them in the Sabbath schools. Professor Heber S. Goddard is now teaching me to sing, "Who's on the Lord's side, Who?" I do not know how many months it will take him, but I propose to learn it some day, whether it takes six months or six years. . . . When I do, if I get the opportunity, I will sing it here. I make these remarks because I feel that we ought to encourage our young people to learn to sing. From the standpoint of a singer, I have lost thirty-three years of my life. I was told when ten years old that I could never learn to sing. I did not learn until forty-three years of age, and I have spent four or five months trying to learn to sing the hymns, "God moves in a mysterious way," and "O My Father." I have learned one because of the sentiments and my love for the author, and the other because the late President Wilford Woodruff loved it better than any other hymn in the hymn book. Now all singers say it is a mistake to speak before you sing, and therefore if I do not sing very well it is because I spoke first (Conference Report, Apr. 1900, 61).

* * *

Evan Stephens: I glory in Brother Grant's pluck in learning to sing, and especially because he had no talent at all. I do not think it was a matter of laughter at all this evening to hear him. I have heard worse singing than that from professionals (Conference Report, Apr. 1901, 83).

* * *

J. Golden Kimball: When I was in California I was very low spirited and broken down in body. . . . One day when I was laying on the sand, near the ocean, I happened to pick up a paper, and it gave me new life and new energy. It was a funny picture; it was a picture of a great big monkey, it represented, "Fate—The Old Monkey." It was an editorial. I haven't it with me, but I have read it a good many times, and I desire to make a comparison. There was a very prominent citizen that had an intelligent monkey. He was a mischievous fellow, and he just went around the house knocking everything down that he could get hold of. He knocked over everything that he came to; he discovered that the things he knocked over did not get up again. He was just as mischievous as fate seems to be with us. Finally, this good citizen took the image of a little man, made of some kind of material, and placed it on a very strong base. It was so arranged that when you knocked it over it would come up again. So he set this little man in the room. The monkey came around, took his right hand and cuffed it over. To his surprise it wobbled a little and staggered, and then rose up and seemingly looked at him. Then he took his other hand and cuffed it again, and it came up again. Then he took the hand of his right leg and knocked it again, and then with his left hind leg; then he got on it with all four hands and took one hand up at a time. To his surprise, the little man rose up. The intelligent monkey almost became a monkey maniac. He kept at it and kept at it until he hated and despised the little man; and whenever they would move the little man near the monkey, he would get off in the corner and chatter and become angry. He wouldn't have anything to do with the little man. The Church of Jesus Christ of Latter-day Saints is similar, or like that little man. You can knock it down one hundred times; you can knock it down one thousand times; it may wobble, but it will rise up again, and it will keep rising up until God has accomplished His work. This is God's work, and I look in sympathy upon men who oppose it (Conference Report, Oct. 1910, 34).

PERSPECTIVE

* J O K E S *

Isn't it funny—when the other fellow takes a long time to do something, he's slow. But when I take a long time to do something, I'm thorough. When the other fellow doesn't do it, he's too lazy. But when I don't do it, I'm too busy. When the other fellow goes ahead and does something without being told, he's overstepping his bounds. But when I go ahead and do something without being told, that's initiative! When the other fellow states his side of a question strongly, he's bullheaded. But when I state a side of a question strongly, I'm being firm. When the other fellow overlooks a few of the rules of etiquette, he's rude. But when I skip a few of the rules, I'm original. When the other fellow does something that pleases the boss, he's polishing the brass. But when I do something that pleases the boss, that's cooperation. When the other fellow gets ahead, he sure had the lucky breaks. But when I manage to get ahead, man! Hard work did that! Funny, isn't it—or is it?

* * *

Ed was having trouble with a tooth and finally decided to visit the dentist.

"It's beyond help," the dentist said. "We're going to have to pull that tooth."

"How much will it cost?" asked Ed.

"Two hundred dollars," answered the dentist.

"Two hundred dollars! For five minutes' work?" asked Ed, outraged.

"Calm down," said the dentist. "I'll make you a deal. If you'd like me to, I'll extract the tooth very slowly."

189

* * *

The day of a big snowstorm, the country schoolteacher felt called upon to warn her charges against playing too long in the snow. She said, "Now, children, you must be careful about colds and over-exposure. I had a darling little brother only seven years old. One day he went out in the snow with his new sled and caught cold. Pneumonia set in, and three days later he died."

The room was silent. Then a youngster in the back row raised his hand and asked, "Where's his sled?"

PHILOSOPHY

* QUOTATIONS *

Marion D. Hanks: Some weeks ago it was my privilege to go into one of the great subterranean caverns in the southwestern part of our land. . . . We came into an area where there was . . . [a] vast vaulted dome, but the debris from that cavity lay below it in a mountainous pile. . . . There were comments along the trail. One said: "My, I'll bet there was a tremendous clap of noise when that fell!" An army man replied, "Do you really think there was? After all, there was no one here to hear it!"

They discussed this issue at some length, whether or not in the absence of someone to hear, noise actually occurs. I listened and said nothing, but thought of Bishop Berkeley, Irish philosopher, whose theory was that "to be is to be perceived," that is, that so-called material things exist only in being perceived—if it is not perceived, it does not exist. It is said that a group of the bishop's students at Oxford taught him the true nature of reality one very dark evening when they placed a tree stump on a certain unlighted path where he habitually walked. His perception of the stump was said to be a realistic shock to George Berkeley (*Improvement Era,* June 1957, 446).

* * *

John Taylor: Speaking of philosophy, . . . I was almost buried up in it while I was in Paris. I was walking about one day in the Jardin des Plantes—a splendid garden. There they had a sort of exceedingly light cake. It was so thin and light that you could blow it away, and you could eat all day of it, and never be satisfied. Somebody asked me what the name of that was. I said, I don't know the proper name, but in the absence of one, I can give it a name—I will call it philosophy, or fried froth, whichever you like. It is so light you can blow it away, eat it all day, and at night be as far from being satisfied as when you began (*Gospel Kingdom,* 78).

* * *

Brigham Young: Now if philosophers will point out where empty space is, I will pay them for their trouble, because all the wicked will be running to me to know where it is, that they may be where God does not dwell, for they will want the rocks and mountains to fall on them to hide them from His presence. I could make money by directing poor devils where empty space is (*Journal of Discourses* 3:279).

PIONEERS

* J O K E S *

Recipe for Making Soup

As provisions are scarce and hard to obtain, we thought it would not be amiss to give our readers the following items to make a good soup. Take a pair of old stoga boots. Carefully skin them and take out the kidney tallow. Cut them into sizeable pieces. Put them into a large iron pot with ten gallons of rain water. As soon as the water is warm, add three quarts of the best shoe pegs you can buy. Also 10–1/2 oz. of Hungarian tacks and a pound of brass buttons. Let it simmer for 2 hours, then add a trace of colts 'revolvers and a quantity of stone cutters mallets' for dumplings. Let it boil for 1 hour. Stir in 5 oz. of indigo for seasoning. To be served up in canteens with 10 penny nails for spoons. To be eaten while hot with nicely browned pieces of an old red flannel shirt (*Veprecula*, 15 May 1864; quoted in Davis Bitton, *Wit and Whimsy in Mormon History*, 28–29).

*   Q U O T A T I O N S   *

Andrew Jenson: I shall never forget my experience in crossing the Atlantic in the ship *Kenilworth* and the plains in Captain Scott's ox team. I have often thanked the Lord that I came that year, and not later. Had I come the next year (1867), I should have been deprived of the privilege of traveling three hundred miles on foot, because that year the railroad had been built that far westward from the Missouri river; and the year following, (1868) it was built more than half way across the plains, and mountains, or as far as Ft. Laramie, and later in the year Ft. Benton, on the upper Platte. The next year (1869) all the fun was over. After that all the immigrants had to travel all the way by rail (Conference Report, Oct. 1916, 114).

POLITICS

* QUOTATIONS *

J. Golden Kimball: For the last few weeks I have been reading platforms and pledges and promises of political parties, which if carried out would suffice for this nation for at least 1,000 years (Conference Report, Oct. 1912, 26).

* STORIES *

"Congress is so strange," commented Boris Marshalov, a Russian actor and dramatic coach, after a visit to the spectators' gallery of the House of Representatives. "A man gets up to speak and says nothing. Nobody listens—and then everybody disagrees."

POWER

* QUOTATIONS *

Brigham Young: We are not the Almighty. I am glad of it. I am happy in the reflection that I have not the power [to destroy the Saints' enemies], and I hope and pray I may never possess it until I can use it like a God, until I can wield it as our Father in heaven wields it, with all that eternity of majesty, glory, charity, with his judgment, discretion, and with every faculty of compassion. I am happy in the reflection that I do not possess the power. I am glad you elders do not, I am really glad you do not (*Journal of Discourses* 15:1–4).

PRAYER

* JOKES *

A little girl had some blocks with letters on them. She was learning the ABCs with the use of her blocks, and one night just before bedtime she was playing with them. When she got into bed she started to say her prayers, but she was so sleepy that all she could say was, "Oh, Heavenly Father, I am too sleepy to say my prayers. Here are the blocks and the letters. You spell it out."

* * *

Little Susie concluded her prayer by saying: "Dear God, before I finish, please take care of Daddy, take care of Mommy, take care of my baby brother, Grandma, and Grandpa . . . and please, God, take care of yourself, or else we're all sunk!"

* * *

A teacher handed out the test papers, then looked around the room after telling the children to begin. One little girl sat with her head down.

"Megan, do you understand the directions?" the teacher asked.

"Yes, ma'am," Megan whispered. "I don't know if it's unconstitutional or not, but I always say a little prayer before I take a test."

* QUOTATIONS *

Charles W. Penrose: I remember a story told of a man who made a bet that a friend of his did not know the Lord's Prayer, and the bet was taken up, the money was deposited, and the man who laid the money down was very confident. When he was asked to repeat the Lord's Prayer he said:

> "Now I lay me down to sleep,
> I pray the Lord my soul to keep;
> And if I die before I wake,
> I pray the Lord my soul to take."

The other man said, "Well, the money is yours; but I didn't believe you could do it" (Conference Report, Oct. 1906, 52).

* * *

Joseph Fielding Smith: Our prayers are not for the purpose of telling [the Lord] how to run his business (*Take Heed to Yourselves!* 343–44).

* * *

Brigham Young: How gladly I would tell the people what to pray for. But if I tell them, in ten minutes afterwards they pray for something else (*Journal of Discourses* 6:46).

* * *

J. Golden Kimball: The father almost needs the patience of Job to get a family together for morning prayer. That is pretty plain talk, but you seem to understand what I mean. I guess you have tried it (Conference Report, Apr. 1913, 89).

* * *

Brigham Young: Do you want to know how to pray in your families? I have told you, a great many times, how to do when you feel as though you have not a particle of the Spirit of prayer with you. Get your wives and your children together, lock the door so that none of them will get out, and get down on your knees; and if you feel as though you want to swear and fight, keep on your knees until they are pretty well wearied (*Journal of Discourses* 4:200).

* **S T O R I E S** *

Once while on assignment to a conference in Southern Utah, President [George Albert] Smith and Arthur [Haycock] stayed at the home of a rancher who raised sheep and turkeys. Very successful in his enterprises, the rancher had little time for observing the Sabbath Day or attending church.

Still, when the two visitors came to breakfast in the morning, all the chairs had been turned out from the table in preparation for family prayer. The rancher's six-year-old boy took one look at the arrangement of chairs and started to giggle. He was obviously trying to figure out how he was going to get his father's attention. But his father hushed him up as President Smith proceeded to kneel and pray. After the prayer, the little boy piped up, "Daddy, what was that man saying to the chair?" (Swinton, *In the Company of Prophets*, 40–41).

* * *

A story is told that while hiding from persecution during the early days of the Church, Elder Heber C. Kimball had to stay in the home of a widow. When he retired to his bedroom, she thought, "Here's the chance to see what wonderful things an apostle says during his prayers," and she listened quietly at his door. She heard him sit on the bed. Then she heard each of his boots drop to the floor. Finally she heard Elder Kimball's prayer: "Oh, Lord, bless Heber, he is so very tired."

* * *

President Dwight D. Eisenhower usually opened his Cabinet meetings with a prayer by Secretary of Agriculture Ezra Taft Benson. On one occasion, however, Eisenhower forgot to do so. When he was reminded of his oversight by Secretary of State Dulles, he remarked, "Oh, no! And I really need all the help we can get from up there this morning."

* * *

In 1974, while attending the open house of the Washington Temple, Spencer W. Kimball was invited to offer the invocation in the United States Senate. Only a few senators were present, however, while most of the others were in a committee meeting. When someone apologized that so few were there to hear the prayer, President Kimball responded, "That's all right. I was not going to pray to them, anyway" (Kimball, "Spencer W. Kimball," *BYU Studies* 25[4]: 68

* * *

Orson F. Whitney: It is a common remark to this day that such prayers are seldom heard as were wont to issue from the heart and lips of Heber C. Kimball. Reverence for Deity was one of the cardinal qualities of his nature. Nevertheless, it was noticeable that the God to whom he prayed was a being "near at hand and not afar off." He worshiped not as "a worm of the dust," hypocritically meek and lowly, or as one conscious of naught but the meanness of his nature and the absence of merit in his cause. But in a spirit truly humble, confessing his sins, yet knowing something of the nobility of his soul, he talked with God "as one man talketh with another"; and often with the ease and familiarity of an old-time friend.

On one occasion, while offering up an earnest appeal in behalf of certain of his fellow creatures, he startled the kneeling circle by bursting into a loud laugh in the very midst of his prayer. Quickly regaining his composure and solemn address, he remarked, apologetically: "Lord, it makes me laugh to pray about some people" (Whitney, *Life of Heber C. Kimball,* 426–27).

PREPAREDNESS

* JOKES *

An enthusiastic woman told a group of friends in delight of the opportunity she had had to apply the knowledge she had acquired in her first aid class. "It was wonderful," she said. "It was so fortunate that I'd had the training. I was crossing Fifth Avenue at 57th Street and heard a crash behind me. I turned around and saw a poor man who had been struck by a taxicab. He had a compound fracture of the leg, was bleeding terribly, was unconscious and seemed to have a fractured skull. Then all my first aid came back to me—and I stooped right down and put my head between my legs to keep myself from fainting!"

PRIDE

* JOKES *

A man all wrapped up in himself makes a very small package.

* * *

A fierce young lion, wanting to establish his leadership, went through the jungle asking the other animals, "Who's king here?"

The first animal, the gazelle, answered, "You, O mighty lion."

The next animal, a chimpanzee, answered the same way: "You, O mighty lion."

The third animal, an irritable old elephant, took the lion in his trunk, whirled him around, and threw him twenty feet. The lion staggered to his feet, brushed himself off, and said shakily, "Just because you don't know the answer doesn't mean you have to lose your temper."

The moral: Pride goeth before a fall, but it goeth a lot quicker after one.

* * *

Two men parachute from an airplane. The first pulls the ripcord, and the chute opens perfectly. The second pulls the cord—and nothing happens. He keeps falling straight down.

As the second man passes his friend, the first guy gets mad, unbuckles his harness, and shouts, "So you wanna race, huh?"

* * *

A young girl came to Father Healey of Dublin and confessed that she feared she had committed the sin of vanity. "What makes you think that?" asked her father confessor.

"Because every morning when I look into the mirror I think how beautiful I am."

"Never fear, my girl," was the reassuring reply. "That isn't sin, it's only a mistake."

* * *

An aspiring author who took himself quite seriously was having lunch with a friend. "Guess whose birthday it is today?" he asked.

"Yours?" guessed the friend.

"Nope, but you're getting close. Shakespeare's."

* * *

Cameron had just moved into his shiny new office and was awaiting his first client. Suddenly he heard footsteps coming down the hall towards his office. He couldn't resist showing off a little; he picked up the phone and began talking to nobody.

"I'm quite busy right now," he said. "Well . . . yes, I see. I could probably work you in sometime next week."

He looked up and saw a man waiting in front of his desk. Then he turned back to his bogus conversation: "What's that? Next Thursday, then? Two o'clock? All right, I'll see you then."

Cameron hung up the phone and looked up at the man waiting to see him. "Hello. And how may I help you?"

"I don't really need any help, sir," the man answered. "I just came to connect your telephone."

* QUOTATIONS *

J. Golden Kimball: I feel a good deal like the story I read the other day. Some fellow was sitting on the pier that reached out into the ocean—and he fell in, and he yelled, "Help! help! I can't swim." And an old fellow was sitting on the pier fishing, and he said: "Neither can I, but I wouldn't brag about it" (Conference Report, Oct. 1922, 170).

* * *

Rudger Clawson: Day before yesterday, I was proud and high-minded and lifted up in my feelings. Through some strange accident, I got hold of the hat of President Penrose and wore it all the afternoon. I am free to confess that I could not fill his shoes, but I filled his hat (Conference Report, Oct. 1922, 180).

* * *

Joseph S. Geddes: Now, I feel, my brethren and sisters, that my time is about up. I am interested in the work of the Lord. My stake is located in southern Idaho. The northern boundary of Utah is our southern line. We are bounded on the south by the Benson stake, on the west by the Malad, on the north by the Pocatello and Bannock, and on the east by the Bear Lake stake; so you see Oneida is located on the map directly in the center of the earth, and all the important stakes are close by and paying tribute to it (Conference Report, Apr. 1914, 64).

* * *

Hugh B. Brown: The Lethbridge Stake, brethren and sisters, comprises the whole of the north end of the world (laughter). The southern boundary of the Lethbridge Stake is fifteen miles north of the international boundary line, between Canada and the United States. I think the northern boundary of our stake is, perhaps, the southern boundary of South America. We have a very large stake, geographically speaking; and I believe, if we were able to discover all of our people there, we would have the largest stake in the Church, numerically speaking, because I believe we have in our stake the Ten Tribes. They are up there somewhere, although we haven't found them yet (Conference Report, Apr. 1922, 106).

* * *

Richard L. Evans: A smart young man had just returned from college, and at the table he wished to show his parents what extraordinary advancement he had made. "Why, father," says he, "you can hardly conceive of the advance I have made."

"Well, my son," says the father, "I am sure I am glad to hear you say so, and I trust you will make a great man."

There happened to be two ducks on the table for dinner, and this young man proposed to give his father a specimen of his smartness.

"Now," he says, "you see there are only two ducks, don't you?"

"Yes," answered the father.

"Well, I can prove to you that there are three ducks."

"Can you?" says the father. "That's quite extraordinary, really. How can you do it?"

"Well," says the son, "I will show you. That's one?" "Yes." "That's two?" "Yes."

"Well, two and one make three, don't they?"

"Quite so," says the father. "It is very extraordinary, and to show you how much I appreciate it, I will eat one of these ducks, and your mother will eat the other, and we will leave the third for you" (Conference Report, Oct. 1943, 38).

*   *   *

H. David Burton: A ship's captain . . . saw what looked like the light of another ship heading toward him. He had his signalman blink to the other ship: "Change your course 10 degrees south." The reply came back, "Change *your* course 10 degrees north." The ship's captain answered: "I am a *captain*. Change *your* course south." To which the reply came, "Well, I am a seaman first class. Change *your* course north." This so infuriated the captain, he signaled back, "I say change *your* course south. I am on a battleship!" To which the reply came back, "And I say change *your* course north. I am in the lighthouse" (*Ensign*, May 1994, 68).

* S T O R I E S *

At age ten Queen Elizabeth II (1926–) of England was at Glamis Castle and received a visit by a preacher. When he was leaving, he promised to send "Lillibet" a book. The future queen replied, "Oh, thank you so much. But please let it be not about God. I know everything about Him."

* * *

Clyde Fitch tells the following story of the famous artist Whistler. Whistler was in Paris at the time of the coronation of King Edward, and at a reception one evening a duchess said to him, "I believe you know King Edward, Mr. Whistler."

"No, madame," replied Whistler.

"Why, that's odd," she murmured, "I met the King at a dinner party last year and he said that he knew you."

"Oh," said the painter, "he was just boasting."

* * *

Oscar Levant is noted for his self-esteem. Occasionally he would tell this story on himself. "Once I was saying to an old friend how remarkable was our congeniality since we had practically nothing in common."

"Oh, but we have, " replied the friend, "I think you're wonderful and you agree with me."

* * *

While D'Annunzio was living in France, a letter was addressed to him simply with the words: "To Italy's Greatest Poet." He declined to accept it, saying that he was not Italy's greatest poet—he was the world's greatest poet.

* * *

Paderewski was once traveling incognito through Germany. He stopped for the night at a small inn in the Black Forest. In the main room of the inn was an old battered piano. Paderewski asked the landlord if he might try it. Upon doing so, he found that the instrument was not only badly out of tune but that a number of the keys were stuck and would strike no sound at all. He remarked upon this to the landlord. The latter, offended at the criticism of his piano, replied, "If you were a good pianist you could skip over those keys so it wouldn't matter."

* * *

One of Emerson's rural neighbors at Concord borrowed from him a copy of Plato. "Did you enjoy the book?" asked Emerson when it was returned.

"I did at that," replied his neighbor. "This Plato has a lot of my ideas."

PRIORITIES

* STORIES *

When Archbishop Patrick J. Ryan of Philadelphia was a very young priest he was stationed at a parish in St. Louis, where Archbishop Kendrick presided over the diocese. The latter lived in a very small, unpretentious house, scarcely in keeping with his position in the church.

One day when Father Ryan was passing the house of the archbishop, accompanied by a Chicago priest who was visiting St. Louis, he pointed out the house as the residence of the head of the local church. The Chicago priest said with surprise:

"Why, you should see the splendid residence we have in Chicago for our archbishop!"

"Yes," said Father Ryan, "but you should see the splendid archbishop we have in St. Louis for our residence."

* * *

Assigned to a conference at the Teton Stake in Idaho, J. Golden Kimball went to visit the stake president at his home. There he saw a fine new barn, abundant crops, and handsome animals, but the house was an old two-room cabin. After the stake president proudly showed him around, Elder Kimball said, "You have a nice home for your horses and cows. Next year when I come, I want to see a nice home for your wife and kids" (Cheney, *Golden Legacy*, 110).

PROBLEMS

* QUOTATIONS *

Ashleigh Brilliant: It's not easy taking my problems one at a time when they refuse to get in line.

PROCRASTINATION

* JOKES *

If it weren't for the last minute, very little would be accomplished in this world.

PROGRESS

* JOKES *

A young girl took a trip to the lake with her family. Watching a water-skier, she said to her mother, "Look at that man. He'll never catch that boat."

*   *   *

A young teenager felt she could do nothing right. Whether it was her chores, her homework, or her eating habits, it seemed her parents and others were always criticizing her. Finally she made a large button and pinned it to her blouse:

"Please be patient. God has not finished with me yet."

* QUOTATIONS *

J. Golden Kimball: We see your red lights, we see your green lights, and the officers of this city are doing everything in their power to protect the people, but the people do not pay any attention to the signals—some of them do not. There is nothing else annoys me so much as for a man to run on to me with one of those great, powerful machines, and just before hitting me, honk his horn. My legs go right from under me. I can't even hit a trot, and the feeling I have is that he is saying: "Get out of the way, we are coming." I got that the other night on First North street here. I can see only one way at a time, and then I am not quite clear, but I had to see four ways that night. Here came two machines around that corner, with these cars all parked right up to the corner, and they tried to beat each other through and caught me in the center. The only thing that saved my life was my being thin (Conference Report, Oct. 1926, 129).

* * *

Mark Twain: Training is everything. The peach was once a bitter almond; the cauliflower is nothing but a cabbage with a college education.

* * *

Joseph Fielding Smith: The people in our land, as well as in foreign lands, are all going crazy over getting to the moon, setting up headquarters there, and so forth. I think the Lord sits in the heavens and laughs at our foolishness. He does not have to do like He did in the days of the building of the Tower of Babel, come down to take a look. But I think he sits in the heavens and smiles at the foolishness of mortal men. Now I did not intend to say that, but I have something I am going to read. . . . I forgot to get the man's name who wrote this:

Twinkle, twinkle, little star,
I don't wonder what you are.
I surmised your spot in space
When you left your missile base.
Any wondering I do
Centers on the price of you.
And I shudder when I think
What you're costing us, each wink.

(*Speeches of the Year*, 25 Oct. 1961, 5).

* * *

Robert L. Simpson: After I had been in New Zealand for just a short time, I went down to a place called Judea, in Tauranga. The mission president said, "I want you to go down there and learn how to speak Maori." He didn't say anything to the branch president, but the branch president had assigned all the Primary children to teach me how to speak Maori. I was helping to build a small chapel. While we were up there hammering nails, these Primary children would sit down on the grass and jabber Maori to me all day. They wouldn't speak any English. They knew how to speak English—they knew more languages than I did. But, they wouldn't answer me if I spoke to them in English. I had to speak Maori to them. They were forcing me to learn this language, that I might be a more effective missionary.

I remember they taught me a little song. Oh, how grateful I was to them! I thought to myself as I was learning this little ditty, "Here I am, learning the great chants of the old Maoris, passed down through hundreds of years. I have just been in New Zealand a few weeks and already I can sing this old time song." I didn't know at the time what it meant, but I will never forget it as long as I live. . . .

Imagine my surprise when I found out it was "Hey diddle diddle, the cat and the fiddle, the cow jumped over the moon"! The world is getting pretty small, and I think that is a fairly good indication (*Speeches of the Year*, 19 Oct. 1965, 3–4).

* * *

Ardeth Greene Kapp: Every year I find myself becoming more and more concerned about health, perhaps because a friend warns me that after forty years of age, it's patch, patch, patch. . . . I heard the other day of a lady much older than I who had completed fifty pushups that very morning. That was distressing to me until I learned that she had begun them a year ago! (*My Neighbor, My Sister, My Friend,* 91).

* STORIES *

Elder Ronald Poelman was returning from a conference in St. Louis on the same plane as President Spencer W. Kimball. When Elder Poelman got up to walk for a minute, President Kimball caught his arm. "Where are you going?" he asked.

"I was just stretching my legs."

"You don't need to do that; they're long enough already. It's little people like me who need to stretch their legs" (Kimball, "Spencer W. Kimball," *BYU Studies* 25[4]: 64).

* * *

When James A. Garfield was president of Hiram College a man brought up his son to be entered as a student. He wanted the boy to take a course shorter than the regular one.

"My son can never take all those studies," said the father. "He wants to get though more quickly. Can't you arrange it for him?"

"Oh, yes," said Mr. Garfield. "He can take a short course; it all depends on what you want to make of him. When God wants to make an oak he takes a hundred years, but he takes only two months to make a squash."

PROPHECY

J. Golden Kimball: I have been told that I should prophesy. I want to say to you Latter-day Saints that to be a prophet of God all fear and all doubt have to leave your mind, and you then open your mouth and God gives you the words. But I have become so fearful about things I would be afraid to let it loose. I want to tell you there are a lot of us in the same fix. We are afraid of what people will think and are doubtful about its fulfillment.

When Heber C. Kimball prophesied that goods would be sold as cheap in the streets of Salt Lake as in New York, he himself turned to President Young and said:

"Brother Young, I think I have made a mistake." Brother Young said: "Never mind, Heber. Let it go."

Charles C. Rich, after the meeting, said: "Heber, I don't believe a word you said."

Heber said: "Neither do I." . . . But he said: "God has spoken." And God had spoken.

No wonder he was frightened, for the people were in the depths of poverty, a thousand miles away from nowhere.

My testimony to you is that those gifts and promises are the heritage of God's children. I am not a visionary man, I am not a dreamer. I sometimes wonder what my gift is. I have never seen an angel, but I have the assurance that comes to me and is burned in my heart like a living fire by the power of the Holy Ghost, that God is the Father, that Jesus is the Christ. I believe with all my soul that Joseph Smith was a prophet and is a prophet of God, and God knows there is ample proof to substantiate it. I also believe that Heber J. Grant is a prophet of God, and whenever God gets ready to give him something to tell you I promise you in the name of the Lord you will get it, and you will get it straight, too (Conference Report, Oct. 1932, 20–21).

* * *

James G. Duffin: I want to call your attention to a remark that was made by a son of Heber C. Kimball, some years ago in speaking at a conference in this great Tabernacle. He said: "If you Latter-day Saints would but put yourselves in a position to fulfill prophecy, after it had been made by the servants of God, they would not be so afraid to prophesy!" (Conference Report, Apr. 1908, 85).

PUNCTUALITY

* JOKES *

The owner of a large fruit stand hired a boy who was required to show up by three o'clock every morning to receive the farmers' deliveries. The owner himself wasn't supposed to arrive until opening time hours later. For the sake of checking up, though, the owner unexpectedly came to his stand at three o'clock one morning and saw that the boy wasn't there. Finally, at 3:05, the boy rushed through the door. "So!" shouted the employer. "Banker's hours!"

* QUOTATIONS *

Times and Seasons: Pres't Washington was the most punctual man in the observance of appointments ever known to the writer. He delivered his communications to Congress at the opening of each session, in person.—He always appointed the hour of twelve for this purpose, and he never failed to enter the hall of Congress while the state-house clock was striking that hour. His invitations for dinner were always given for four o'clock, P.M. He allowed five minutes for variation of time pieces, and he waited no longer for any one. Certain lagging members of Congress sometimes came in when the dinner was nearly half over. The writer has heard the President say to them with a smile, "gentlemen we are too punctual for you—I have a cook who never asks whether the company has come, but whether the hour has come" (*Times and Seasons*, 2:270).

* * *

Ezra Taft Benson: Orson F. Whitney . . . was a great man to concentrate. One day when he was traveling by train, he was so preoccupied that he did not notice the train pass the station where he was to get off. So he had to [be driven] back to where he should have been. Meanwhile the stake president waited and waited. . . . Finally when he decided that something had more than likely happened to Brother Whitney and he was not going to make it, they commenced the meeting. As Elder Whitney approached, he was greeted by the opening hymn, which was "Ye Simple Souls Who Stray" (*Ensign*, May 1993, 39).

PURPOSE

* QUOTATIONS *

J. Golden Kimball: I have worked in the Church, perhaps not as well as I might have done, but I have staked everything on it. As I told a man one day, I had fifty-two cards in the beginning. I never played cards in my life—only smut. But to illustrate: I am not a card player, but in the beginning I had fifty-two of them—that is a deck, I think. Some of you seventies are better informed, perhaps, than I, but at the present time I have only one card left. Do you know what I have staked it on? Eternal life; and if I fail in that I have failed in everything. Why? Because "salvation is the greatest gift of God to his children." Of all the gifts and all the blessings that God can give to his children, the "greatest gift is salvation." If you leave your father and if you leave your mother, your wife and your children, and your flocks and your herds, and all that you have, and go out as a witness for God, he has promised you an hundred fold. All the investments I ever made in my life, except the one of two Liberty Bonds I have been able to pay for, at four per cent, I have paid from eighteen per cent down, and all I got out of it was experience; the other fellow got my money. . . . But this investment we have started out for, the Lord has promised you an hundred fold, and I pray God that this spirit may burn in the hearts of the priesthood of God (Conference Report, Oct. 1918, 31).

* S T O R I E S *

When David O. McKay was nearly fourteen, he received his patriarchal blessing, in which he was told that he would sit in council with his brethren and preside among the people. After giving the blessing, the stake patriarch rested his hands on David's shoulders and said, "My boy, you have something to do besides playing marbles."

Apparently young David did not grasp the full import of his blessing. He went into the kitchen, where he found his mother preparing dinner, and announced, "If he thinks I'm going to stop playing marbles, he is mistaken" (see Morrell, *Highlights from the Life of David O. McKay*, 26).

RECREATION

* Q U O T A T I O N S *

Richard Eyre: We took a business associate to our [favorite] lake for a long weekend one summer. He spent the first day worrying about the calls he couldn't make since we had no phone. The second day he gave in a little and started relaxing and enjoying himself. At the end of the third day he said, "You know, I think I've forgotten how to play." Then a pause and smile. "But I'm starting to think I have a natural aptitude for it and can relearn it if I just apply myself" (*Don't Just Do Something: New Maxims to Refresh and Enrich Your Life*, 39).

RELIGION

* J O K E S *

An agnostic and an atheist got married and got along fine until they began to have children. Then they began to have many heated arguments. They couldn't decide which religion not to raise their children in.

REPENTANCE

* JOKES *

Reading the paper one morning, a man was startled to find his name on the obituary page. He quickly called the editor to protest. "I'm awfully sorry," the editor replied. "And it's too late to do much about it. The best thing I can do for you is to put you in the 'Birth Column' tomorrow morning, and give you a fresh start."

* * *

An elderly sister wanted to get her temple recommend renewed—and she planned to tell the bishop about all her shortcomings. To make sure she didn't forget anything, she wrote it down on a list. When she got to the bishop's office that Tuesday night, she handed him the paper. "Here's what I need to talk to you about," she said.

The bishop glanced down at the paper. "Eggs?" he said. "Cheese?"

The woman grabbed the paper back, looked at it, and exclaimed, "Good gracious! I must have left my sins at the grocery store!"

* * *

A young man inherited his uncle's very intelligent Amazon parrot. The parrot was no prize, however; he had a bad attitude and a worse vocabulary. It seemed that every other word was either an expletive or extremely rude. The nephew tried everything he could think of—talking sweetly to the parrot, playing soft music on the radio, making sure the bird could hear conference and the weekly Tabernacle Choir broadcast.

None of it made a bit of difference. If he yelled at the parrot, the parrot squawked back. If he shook it, it bit him. If he asked politely, the bird mimicked his nice words but interspersed them with profanities.

Finally, absolutely exasperated, the nephew stuck the parrot in the freezer. "This will teach him a thing or two," he said.

The bird kicked and banged and squawked and swore—then, suddenly, turned quiet. The nephew listened, worried and expectant. There wasn't a sound. Oh, no! he thought. Have I killed my uncle's parrot? He quickly flung open the freezer door. The parrot stepped out onto his outstretched arm. "I must say," the parrot said, "I am truly sorry that I have offended you with my language and my attitude. Please forgive me. I assure you I will never behave in such a manner again."

The nephew was amazed. How could the bird have changed so suddenly and so completely? He was about to ask when the parrot continued. "I have just one question. May I ask what the chicken did?"

*   Q U O T A T I O N S   *

J. Golden Kimball: I thank God the Eternal Father that up to the present I have had the spirit of repentance, and while it has kept me pretty busy repenting, I hope I will always have that spirit (Conference Report, Oct. 1910, 31).

*   S T O R I E S   *

A young boy came down to breakfast one morning and said, "Dad, I dreamed about you last night."

"About me? What did you dream?"

"I dreamed I was climbing a ladder to heaven, and on the way up I had to write one of my sins on each step of the ladder."

"Where did I come into your dream?" the father asked.

"When I was going up, I met you coming down for more chalk" (see *New Era,* Jan. 1973, 22).

REPUTATION

* QUOTATIONS *

J. Golden Kimball: I remember something I said once; I tried to forget it, but it got in the Associated Press, and it went all over the land. It is the only time I ever did get any notoriety. The grave question was, did he say it? I could not help but think of the young man who opened this meeting by prayer, of his own volition he got the signatures of eighteen men, intelligent men, business men, who signed a document to the effect that I did not say it. But the word had gone out that I did say it. Some of the brethren said, "Well, it sounded like him." Another good brother that wanted to help me out, said, "He did not say it, but he was not wise." That good brother killed me right there. You let it go out only once, among the children of men, that you are not wise, and you might just as well go off and die (Conference Report, Apr. 1911, 68).

* * *

John M. Knight: One of our reverend gentlemen from this state visited the Western States mission and he magnified greatly the statements that were given by Dr. Martin. He not only said that President Grant controlled millions, but billions of dollars—I think four billions of dollars that he controlled in actual money. I presume he would like to get his hands upon it. This good gentleman applauded our efforts as missionaries. He told of our wonderful organizations. He spoke a good word for the Sabbath schools of the Church of Jesus Christ of Latter-day Saints. He referred to the loyalty of the Saints in observing the law of tithing, and after saying a number of good things he asked the question: "What can we do to stop it?" (Conference Report, Oct. 1922, 42).

RESPONSIBILITY

* JOKES *

This is a story about four people named Everybody, Somebody, Anybody, and Nobody.

There was an important job to be done and Everybody was sure that Somebody would do it.

Anybody could have done it, but Nobody did it.

Somebody got angry about that because it was Everybody's job.

Everybody thought Anybody could do it, but Nobody realized that Everybody wouldn't do it.

It ended up that Everybody blamed Somebody when Nobody did what Anybody could have done.

RESURRECTION

* QUOTATIONS *

Orson Pratt: We are in the habit of taking knives or razors and paring our nails every little while, so much that we can safely say that in the course of a year we cut off or pare from our fingers and toes, as the case may be, perhaps an inch of nail, at this rate, a man who lives to be seventy-two years of age would pare off seventy-two inches of nail, which would be six feet. Now can we suppose than when a man rises from the dead that he will come forth with nails six feet long? . . . I cannot conceive any such thing, and yet this is a portion of the body, and men, in the resurrection, will have nails the same as they have here, but I expect they will be of a reasonable length, and a sufficient portion of the nails of his fingers and toes will be resurrected to make handsome comely nails on the fingers and toes, while all the rest will be surplus and unnecessary (*Journal of Discourses* 16:357).

REVERENCE

* QUOTATIONS *

Brigham Young: While I attempt to speak to the people I would like their attention, and for them to keep quiet. I do not particularly object to the crying of children, but I do to the whispering of the people. I suppose that, if we were in the congregations of some of our Christian fellow-countrymen, we would not hear any children crying. I believe they have none in some societies. I am very happy to hear the children crying when it is really necessary and they cannot be kept from it. One thing is certain, wherever we go there is a proof that the people are keeping the commandments of the Lord, especially the first one—to multiply and replenish the earth (*Journal of Discourses* 13:300).

* * *

Ruth B. Wright: Sister Wilson carefully studied each young child as she entered the Primary classroom. *How they have grown and developed since January,* she thought. She gathered them around her and began her lesson. "You are each very special! You have learned so many things. You have learned to sit reverently and listen to our lessons. Why, you can even say your own prayers!"

"Well, of course," responded Clayton, "I've already been on this earth five years!" (*Ensign*, May 1994, 84).

SABBATH

* J O K E S *

Wife: Now, dear, don't get any ideas about playing golf today. I know it's a beautiful, sunny Sunday, but we have lots of yard work to do.
Husband: Sweetheart! I'm not even remotely thinking about golf. Let's finish up breakfast and get going on that work. Now, would you please pass the putter?

* S T O R I E S *

A man tested the Sabbath years ago by selecting ten acres of his Ohio farm land and plowing, planting, and cultivating his crop in that field entirely on the Sabbath. At the end of October he discovered he had a higher yield, more bushels to the acre, in that field than any other farmer in Ohio had reported. He wrote a letter to the editor of the *Toledo Blade* to boast of his accomplishment. The wise editor printed the letter but then added his own editorial comment: "Remember, my brother, God Almighty does not always settle his accounts in October" (Ayre, *Illustrations to Inspire*, 83).

SATAN

* QUOTATIONS *

Ben E. Rich: It is the work of the adversary to try to creep in between that individual and the people of God. That has always been the work of the evil one; and he holds out false promises to the people as an inducement to get them to turn their backs upon the prophet of Almighty God, just as he held out false promises to the Savior Himself when he . . . showed Him the glories of the world and promised to give them all to Him, if He would fall down and worship him. The old sinner never owned a foot of it (Conference Report, Apr. 1910, 92).

SCHOOL

* JOKES *

A clever schoolteacher sent home a note to the parents of her new students on the first day of school. It read, "If you promise you won't believe everything your child says happens at school, I promise I won't believe everything she says happens at home."

* * *

Child to mother: Guess what? My teacher thinks I'm going to be famous someday!
Mom: Really?
Child: Yup. She said if I get in trouble one more time I'm history!

SCRIPTURE

* J O K E S *

Scholars disagree—does the Bible set a precedent for food fights or for "toilet papering" someone's house? Wrote Zechariah, "Then I turned, and lifted up mine eyes, and looked, and behold a flying roll. And he said unto me, What seest thou? And I answered, I see a flying roll" (Zech. 5:1–2).

* * *

Q. What is Laman and Lemuel's favorite TV show?
A. Diagnosis: Murmur.

Q. When people go past Temple Square, why do they like to look up to Moroni?
A. Because he's always on the ball.

Q. Why did the Lamanites have bruised knees?
A. Because of all the Nephites.

Q. How do we know that Ether was a little dentist?
A. Because he "dwelt in a cavity."

Q. Where do Lamanites go to dance?
A. To Laman Nite clubs.

Q. What was the name of Nephi's horse?
A. Beunto—Nephi called out to him, "Whoa, Beunto" (2 Ne. 28:24–29).

* * *

A little boy asked his grandfather, "Why do you spend so much time reading the scriptures?"

"Well, my boy," answered the grandpa, "I guess you could say I'm cramming for the final examination."

* * *

An elderly woman had just returned to her home from home-making meeting when she was startled by an intruder. "Stop," she yelled. "Acts 2:38." The burglar turned and pointed his gun at her, but she yelled again "Stop! Acts 2:38." The man dropped his gun to the floor and raised his hands to the air. He didn't move an inch while the woman called the police and explained what she had done.

As the officer handcuffed the man to take him in, he asked him, "Why did you give up so easily? All the old lady did was yell a scripture to you."

"Scripture!" the burglar exclaimed, "I thought she said she had an ax and two 38s."

* * *

A sister in the ward asked the bishopric to stop by her home to help her. When they came, she poured out her troubles. Finally the bishop said, "Sister Peters, there's a scripture I'd like to share with you. Can you get your copy?"

Sister Peters called to her young daughter, who was playing in the next room, "Amber, will you please bring me that dear old book I read every night?"

Amber was back in a flash—holding a copy of *TV Guide*.

* * *

Question: Don't you think the scriptures should be rewritten?
Answer: No, they should be reread.

* QUOTATIONS *

J. Golden Kimball: I am going to read to you a little that has been culled from the Bible as to the mission of Christ. I would quote it, but I never dare quote scripture, for after I get through quoting you wouldn't recognize it.

I am a little like father, when he used to quote scripture, he would say, "Well, if that isn't in the Bible, it ought to be in it" (Conference Report, Oct. 1910, 31–32).

* * *

Orson F. Whitney: I had a conversation with another would-be censor of our sacred books. He accosted me on the street with the question: "Bishop Whitney, do you believe the Book of Mormon to be the word of God?" "I certainly do," said I. "Well, can't God speak grammatically?" "Of course he can." "Then why was this grammatical error left in the Book of Mormon?"—and he quoted it. "Do you really want to know?" "Yes," he said. "Well, I think that was left there just to keep you out of the Church."

He seemed surprised: "Doesn't God want me in his Church?" "No," I said; "he only wants honest seekers after truth; and if you think more of a grammatical error than you do of your soul's salvation, you are not fit for the kingdom of heaven, and the Lord doesn't want you."

He was astonished. It was something he hadn't thought of. He felt very much as Goliath did when the stone sank into his fore-head—such a thing had never entered his head before (Conference Report, Apr. 1926, 34–35).

* * *

Richard L. Evans: There are some who come and say they have not been taught, that they wish they had known differently. But the commandments are pretty plain. I would not worry too much about the obscure passages of scripture. We will not be held accountable for things we do not know, but we will be for those we do know.

(I think of a sentence from Mark Twain. One would always expect a bit of humor from him, and there is something of whimsy in this sentence of his: "The scripture passages that bother me the most are the ones I understand." I think we do not need to worry too much about the ones we do not understand) (Conference Report, Apr. 1958, 77).

* S T O R I E S *

Heber J. Grant: I happened to be the chairman of the committee that raised their proportion of the six-billion-dollar fund during the [first] World War. . . . There was a great meeting held in California, and the presidents of the various state organizations of defense and the chairmen of the Liberty Loan drive were invited to that meeting. . . . In that brief meeting there were many doubts expressed as to the war's being won by the allies. I said: "So far as the Mormons are concerned we have no fear whatever as to the outcome. Every Mormon believes in the Book of Mormon, and the Book of Mormon teaches that this is a land choice above all other lands, and that no king, or kaiser for that matter, will ever reign here."

Several said, "My gracious, we had better join the Mormon Church" (see Grant, *Gospel Standards,* comp. Durham, 242).

* * *

In one Primary's sharing time, the students played a "Who Am I?" game using a figure from each of the standard works. The answer to the "Who Am I?" for the Book of Mormon was the Brother of Jared, which the students finally guessed. "But what is his real name?" the teacher asked. "It's long and hard to pronounce." Without hesitation, one of the boys on the back row called out, "John Jacob Jingleheimer Schmidt!"

225

* * *

One evening a sister missionary called her district leader in tears.

Sister missionary: Oh, Elder, I think we really lost our golden investigators this evening!

District leader: What's the matter, Sister?

Sister missionary: Well, in our discussion tonight, we challenged them to read in the Book of Mormon. But instead of asking them to start with 1 Nephi 3:7, I mistakenly asked them to read 3 Nephi 3:7.

District leader: What could be so bad about that?

Sister missionary: Oh, Elder! The first words this investigator is going to read in the Book of Mormon are "Yield yourselves up unto us, and unite with us and become acquainted with our secret works, and become our brethren that ye may be like unto us—not our slaves, but our brethren and partners in all our substance."

* * *

One family experimented with different times to read scriptures together. They tried dinner time, bedtime, and right after school. None of their efforts worked very well. Finally they decided to do it first thing in the morning, at 7:00 A.M., before everybody left for school.

On the first day of their new schedule, Dad had a hard time getting the kids up. He poked and prodded and pulled, tickled and sang and finally shouted. At last they all dragged into the living room, in various stages of disarray, opened their pages, and began at the top of the page. It was Dad's turn to start, and he read,

"Awake! and arise from the dust, and hear the words of a trembling parent, whose limbs ye must soon lay down in the cold and silent grave" (2 Ne. 1:14).

* * *

One of Abraham Lincoln's favorite stories concerned a housewife who would not purchase a Bible from a traveling minister; she claimed she already had a Bible. When the minister asked her to show him the book, the housewife and her son looked all over and finally found only a very few worn pages of the Bible.

The woman would not change her story that she had a Bible, but she did say to the minister, "I had no idea we were so nearly out."

S ELFISHNESS

* J O K E S *

Math teacher: Ryan, if you had six donuts, and I asked you for three, how many would you have left?

Ryan: Six.

* * *

Interviewing a member of his ward, the bishop asked, "If you had two houses, would you give one to a homeless person?"

"I think I would," the man replied.

"If you had two cars, would you give one to someone who needed it?"

"I think I would," the man said.

"If you had two bicycles, would you give one to someone who needed it?"

"No, I don't think so."

"Why not?"

"Well, I *have* two bicycles."

* QUOTATIONS *

John Taylor: As Latter-day Saints, we are sometimes apt to think that we must look after ourselves individually. We are a good deal like the man who, when praying, said—"God bless me and my wife, my son John and his wife, us four and no more, amen." There was no philanthropy, benevolence or kind feeling towards the rest of mankind there, and too many of us feel a good deal in the same way (*Journal of Discourses* 17:212–13).

* * *

George Q. Morris: I was told the other day (I did not learn any more of the details) that a bishop invited some of the members of his ward to a banquet, and as one man had his plate presented to him there was on it a small piece of meat and a small piece of carrot. I do not know what the man's impressions were or what questions arose in his mind, but it was explained to him that that represented the fast offering that he had been giving to the needy. . . . Now that was surely a very realistic way of pointing out his relation to the fast offering and his obligations (*Improvement Era,* June 1957, 425).

SELF-RELIANCE

* QUOTATIONS *

J. Golden Kimball: I am very thankful this morning, notwithstanding the condition of my physical body, that I have been busily engaged cleaning up my own door-yard. I could not get the boy to do it, so I got busy and did it myself (Conference Report, Apr. 1914, 110).

* * *

Joseph F. Smith: The brethren who will follow, through the conference, will be led by the Spirit of the Lord. . . . We expect them to
speak about home industry, for if any people in the world should
believe in the propriety and necessity of home industry, it is the
Latter-day Saints. On the back of that, if there is a people anywhere
in the intermountain region, or anywhere else, who have failed more
completely in maintaining and supporting some kinds of home industry, than we have, I do not know them. . . . Every one of these institu-
tions has gone by the board; because labor was a little higher here,
and cloth could not be produced here quite as cheap, within a few
cents per yard, as the shoddy that is produced in the east could be
made and sent here. We preferred the shoddy to the real goods, and
we bought the shoddy and wore it, and let home manufacture go to
the wall, and yet we believe in home manufacture! . . . I do not want
to boast, but I want to tell you that I have the honor of wearing part
of the last piece of home-made goods produced in Utah. I look about
as well as some of you in your shoddy. (Laughter.) . . .

John R. Winder: I am proud to say, my brethren and sisters, without boasting at all, that I have the honor and the pleasure of wearing
a coat, this morning, made from the same piece of cloth that the
President's coat was made from, (laughter) and I leave you to judge
as to how I look. . . .

Francis M. Lyman: In regard to home industries: I thought I had
the last suit myself, President. (Laughter.) I thought, I had the last silk
that was produced in Utah; and I thought I had the last cloth made
at Provo; but I do not know how many *last pieces* have been made.
(Laughter.) But here is the last silk ever made in Utah, (displaying a
handkerchief.) . . .

Joseph F. Smith: I don't want Brother Lyman to think he has the
last silk handkerchief; (laughter) I have a number of them at home
(Conference Report, Oct. 1909, 6–7, 10, 19–21).

* * *

Brigham Young: You hear the remark that such and such a man is not fit to be a Bishop? I acknowledge that many who are called to be Bishops are not fit for the office, for it is one of the most important offices in the Church to rightly administer in temporal things. A Bishop also ministers in spiritual things, and is required to devote time to the wellbeing and prosperity of his ward, like a father to a family. It is an office that keenly tries the patience, faith, and feelings of a man. If the brethren and sisters prayed for that man continually, and lived their religion, he would know how to settle certain business transactions without running to me about this, that, and the other. Brethren would not run to me about things as simple as, "So-and-so has been building a fence on the line between us, and has put his polls wrong end foremost. Will you not counsel him to turn them?" And sisters are running to me about things as simple as, "Sister So-and-so's hens have laid on my premises, and they do not lay with their heads in the right direction." Does such conduct proceed from true knowledge among the Latter-day Saints? No. I do not wish to talk about such folly, neither to have my time wasted by visits upon such unimportant subjects. I do not wonder that the Lord suffers us to be more or less abused by our enemies. I do not wonder that the devils laugh at our folly (*Journal of Discourses* 7:279).

* * *

Heber J. Grant: We all have temptations, we all have things come into our lives—which if we give them proper consideration, we will reject.

Brother Ballard has referred to the invitation that was sent to President Ivins to accept the nomination as governor of the state of Utah, which reminds me that a telegram came to me from Ogden at that time asking me where they could find Anthony W. Ivins. It said, "We will nominate him by acclamation to be the first governor of the state of Utah or the first representative to Congress."

I answered to the effect that he was on the Kaibab mountain and had accepted a call to go to Mexico. Nothing in the world would cause him to fail to fulfil that call.

I received another telegram telling me that they could not nominate me by acclamation, but that they had the majority pledged to me, and believed it would be by acclamation before the voting was through.

I showed the telegram to Heber M. Wells, who had been nominated by the Republicans. He said: "Well, my name is 'Dennis', the people don't know me. You are sure to be elected."

I said: "Well, I am not sure that I am going to run, I will let you know later."

I went to President Wilford Woodruff and handed him the telegram. I said: "How shall I answer that?"

He said: "What are you bothering me with your affairs for? Haven't you got enough inspiration as one of the Apostles to know what your duty is?"

I said: "Thank you. If you had wanted me to run, you would have said so. Good-bye" (Conference Report, Oct. 1934, 125–26).

* * *

Joseph F. Smith: We ought to live within our means if possible, and if it is not possible and we keep living beyond our means, it is only a question of time when we won't trust us, and we will have to live within our means or die, or steal, as some one has added. When it comes to that kind of thing I feel as Dr. [Samuel] Johnson did when the beggar accosted him, "Why don't you go to work?" said the Doctor. "I cannot get any work, I cannot get anything to do, and you know, Doctor, I must live." "Well," said the Doctor, "I don't see the least necessity for it" (*Journal of Discourses* 25:247–48).

SELF-RIGHTEOUSNESS

* QUOTATIONS *

Humorist H. L. Mencken defined Puritanism as "the lurking, lingering fear that somewhere, someone may be happy."

SERVICE

* JOKES *

A mother was teaching her little son about service. "We need to remember," she explained, "that we're here on earth to help others."

The little boy looked puzzled. "But, Mommy," he asked, "Why are the others here?"

* * *

For the fourth time, Henry came home from school with a black eye. Disappointed, his mother said, "Oh, Henry, you've been fighting again."

"But, Mom," he sniffled, "I was just trying to keep a little boy from getting beaten up by a bigger one."

"Well, that's different," said his mother. "What little boy was that?"

"Me, Mommy."

* * *

There is a story that tells of a rabbit being chased by a dog, and the people following and telling the rabbit to run hard and escape.

"Thank you for you kind encouragement," said the rabbit, "but for goodness' sake stop the dog."

* * *

A Cub Scout troop was half an hour late to its den meeting. The den mother asked them severely, "Why are you so late?"

"Oh," said one boy, "we were helping an old man cross the street."

"That's a nice thing for Scouts to do," said the mother. She paused. "But it shouldn't make you half an hour late."

"Well, you see," said another boy, "he didn't want to go."

* * *

Widow: Thank you, Trent. I'll get on the phone right away and thank your mother for sending you over with these six big blueberry muffins.

Trent: Sister Jones, . . . when you call my mother, could you possibly thank her for those *twelve* muffins?

* * *

Visiting teacher (over the phone): How are you doing?

Woman: Not very well. I have a terrible cold, and yesterday I sprained my arm, so I can't do a thing.

Visiting teacher: You poor thing. Why don't you let me bring dinner over? What time does Fred get home?

Woman: Fred?

Visiting teacher: Your husband.

Woman: My husband's name is Larry.

Visiting teacher: Oh! I must have the wrong number.

Woman: Does that mean you won't be bringing dinner over?

* Q U O T A T I O N S *

Matthew Cowley: Believe it or not, I'm a cook. I stopped it lately because I sample everything I cook. That doesn't help my diet. But nothing would please me more than to have my bishop call me up and say, "Brother Cowley, this is an emergency; we have a sister up here with a family of children; the husband's an invalid; and she has to be with him all the time. How about coming up and cooking the dinner for the next three nights?" I don't know how long that invalid would last, but I'd be glad to go up (*Matthew Cowley Speaks,* 304).

* * *

Derek A. Cuthbert: I think of dear Sister Amy Gent, whom I was privileged to visit for several years as branch president, home teacher, and friend. The first time I visited her, she was 87 years of age. Widowed twice, she was the only member of the Church in her extended family. Was she lonely? Never!

. . . Once she asked me to bring her some missionary tracts, which I thought were to vary her reading. I gave them to her saying, "You will enjoy reading these, Sister Gent."

"Oh, they are not for me," she replied. "I visit an old lady, and I want to share the gospel with her!" (*New Era,* Nov. 1985, 49).

* * *

Ardeth Greene Kapp: One day I . . . was in a second grade elementary classroom. The student-teacher held the children captive with her storytelling skills. In great detail she told of a cross old man whose name was Mr. Black. In contrast, the account was given . . . of a Mr. Brown who was kind and thoughtful and loved by everyone. At the conclusion of the story, the teacher asked the children, "How many of you would like to be a neighbor to Mr. Brown?" Every hand was raised high. Then almost as an afterthought, she inquired if there was anyone who would like to have Mr. Black for a neighbor.

A little boy in a faded green shirt near the back of the room began to raise his hand, which brought a ripple of quiet amusement from the children. . . . When called on for an explanation to his single vote, he spoke in a soft tone. "Well," he said, "I'd like Mr. Black to be my neighbor, because if he was, my mom would make a cake for me to take to him, and then he wouldn't be that way anymore." A hush fell over the room. Everyone felt something wonderful that they couldn't explain. A little child broke the silence like a benediction: "Oh, I wish I'd said that!" (*New Era,* Apr. 1982, 44).

* S T O R I E S *

Spencer W. Kimball seldom helped in the kitchen, but once a neighbor came in while he was drying the dishes. He said, "Saundra, I want you to be sure to write in your journal that I did the dishes for Camilla" (Kimball, "Spencer W. Kimball," *BYU Studies* 25[4]: 64).

* * *

In Arizona, Spencer W. Kimball sometimes visited "Grandma" Craig, an elderly woman who was one of his many friends, always joking that he was the Fuller Brush man. Years later, when she was her on her deathbed, he came to say good-bye. At first she didn't recognize him. But when he mentioned Fuller brushes, she smiled and pressed his hand (Kimball, "Spencer W. Kimball," *BYU Studies* 25[4]: 61).

SHARING

* JOKES *

Primary teacher: If your mother gave you a big chocolate chip cookie and a small chocolate chip cookie and asked you to share with your brother, which cookie would you give him?

Jake: That depends. Are you talking about my big brother or my little brother?

SICKNESS

* JOKES *

Doctor to sick man: Well, Herman, I'm sorry to say it. You don't have more than six months to live.

Herman: Six months! I could never pay my doctor bill in just six months!

Doctor: Well, all right. I guess I could give you another six months then.

* STORIES *

Orange Wight (son of Lyman), heard his father describe the escape of Joseph Smith and others from the Missouri jails and their successful flight to the safety of Illinois, including this anecdote: "They all changed their names and started out as land seekers, men

236

from the East hunting homes. They left the main road and traveled through the sparsely settled country on by-roads and at times without a road. . . .

"Now with all their trouble they at times had some amusements. . . . They came to a ranch in an out-of-the-way place and stopped for the night. [They] told their names [fictitious ones]. The next morning they were looking about and walking around, all but Bro. McRay, who was in the house. The proprieter came in and asked his name, said he had forgotten it. And Bro. McRay had also forgotten it—and it had the effect to cause Bro. McRay to take a terrible cramp in his stomach; it came near throwing him into spasms.

"The man ran out where some of the other brethren were and told them that their friend was sick. They went in and said, 'Mr. Brown, what is the matter with you? What have you been eating?' That relieved Mr. Brown to such an extent that he began to get better right away" (*BYU Studies* 13[1]: 6–7).

* * *

After surgery on his vocal cords, Spencer W. Kimball gained a new voice, soft and hoarse and instantly recognizable. One evening Ned Winder, who worked with the Church missionary committee, called him about a mission problem. Having caught a cold, he apologized for his hoarseness, but Elder Kimball responded, "Who is this?" When Brother Winder repeated his name, Elder Kimball responded, "For a minute I thought that I was on both ends of the line" (Kimball, "Spencer W. Kimball," *BYU Studies* 25[4]: 66).

* * *

Spencer W. Kimball had to take several kinds of medication for various conditions, but he didn't like the fact. When his son suggested that he take some aspirin for pain, he replied, "I don't want to take any more pills; I'm already the 'piller' of the Church" (Kimball, "Spencer W. Kimball," *BYU Studies* 25[4]: 66).

SIMPLICITY

* QUOTATIONS *

George Albert Smith: When a man uses ten or fifteen superfluous words to convey one simple idea, his real meaning is lost, he reaches beyond all the rules of grammar and rhetoric, and his idea, which, had it been clothed with simple and appropriate language, might have been good, is lost for want of more suitable words. It is like Massa Gratian's wit—"two grains of wheat hid in three barrels of chaff." It is my advice that our Elders should study brevity in all their discourses and communications to the people, and that they should speak in the plainest and simplest manner. . . . They are like the young gentleman who had just come from college and was desirous of making a considerable show, so when he stopped at a country hotel, he gave the following orders to the ostler—"You will extricate the quadruped from the vehicle, stabulate him, donate him an adequate supply of nutritious aliment, and when the Aurora of man shall illumine the celestial horizon I will award thee a pecuniary compensation."

The lad went into the house to the old man, crying—"Landlord, there is a [foreigner] out here; I can't understand a word he says, do come and talk to him yourself" (*Journal of Discourses* 3:25–26).

SIN

* JOKES *

Farmer Jones was a simple-minded man with an exceptionally beautiful horse named Star. One day he rode the horse into town, tied him to the hitching post, and went into the variety store.

While he was inside, two thieves came by. They knew they couldn't just take the horse—Farmer Jones would report it to the sheriff—so they decided to trick the old farmer. One stole the horse and the other slipped the halter over his neck and remained by the post.

When the farmer emerged from the store, the thief immediately spoke up. "Good farmer," he said, "don't be dismayed that your horse is gone. *I* am your horse. Years ago I sinned and for my sins I changed into a horse. But today my punishment is over, and I can be released if you will allow it."

Farmer Jones was astounded by the story, but with a good heart he sent the man away, wishing him luck in his new life.

The next week Farmer Jones went to a horse auction in a neighboring town, looking for a new horse. There, to his amazement, was his horse, available to the highest bidder! The farmer stared at the horse for a long time to make sure he wasn't mistaken, then finally walked over and whispered in the horse's ear. "So, Star—you've sinned again."

* STORIES *

Although Brigham Young appeared to be serious-minded and firm, he also loved a good time. He was jovial and fun-loving, and his sense of humor endeared him to the Saints.

To an embittered woman who had written him asking that her name be removed from the records of the Church he dictated the following: "Madam . . . I have this day examined the records of baptism for the remission of sins in the Church . . . and not being able to find [your name] recorded therein, I was saved the necessity of erasing your name therefrom. You may therefore consider that your sins have not been remitted you and you can enjoy the benefits thereof" (West, *Profiles of the Presidents*, 72–73).

SPEAKING

* J O K E S *

A Sunday School teacher asked one of her little students to briefly tell the biblical story of Elisha and the bear. "All right," she said. "Elisha had a bear and the children made fun of him, and he said, 'If you make fun of me, I'll set the bear at you, and it will eat you up.' And they did, and he did, and it did."

* * *

A young girl said to her friend after a spelling test, "Sure, I know how to spell banana; I just don't know when to stop."

* * *

A newly sustained bishop and his young wife had a long talk about being supportive of each other. "I need you to be more positive about my talks," he said.

"And I need you to back me up more when I discipline the kids," she answered.

They agreed, but the wife made one further stipulation: "You must never look in the shoebox in the attic."

Many years later, after fifty years of marriage, their children threw a huge party at their home to celebrate the anniversary. During all those years, they had kept their agreement—but on this night, when the bishop went to the attic to get some chairs for their guests, the temptation was suddenly too great. He lifted the lid. Inside were three eggs and $10,000 in cash. What could it mean? He couldn't figure it out. He closed the box and went downstairs with the chairs.

Late in the evening, after the guests were gone, the bishop sat down with his wife. "Honey, I have a confession to make," he said. "I looked in the box."

"Oh, it's okay," his wife said. "But I'm sorry you learned the secret."

"But I don't know what it means," he answered.

"Well, you remember our agreement all those years ago. I resolved I would never be critical of one of your talks. But I also told myself than whenever you gave a real yawner, I would put an egg in the box."

"Oh, my," the bishop said, greatly relieved. "Fifty years and only three eggs. That's not bad at all. But what about the $10,000?"

"Well," the wife answered, gently taking his hand, "every time I got a dozen eggs I sold them."

* * *

If you keep your mouth shut, you'll get credit for knowing what you're talking about.

* * *

Isn't it wonderful how the moment you get up in the morning, the mind begins working, and it doesn't quit until you stand up to give a talk in sacrament meeting?

* * *

The sacrament meeting speaker got sick and canceled out at the last minute, so the bishop called upon a visiting high councilor to speak in his place. The speaker began by discussing the word *substitute*. "When you break a window and then place a piece of cardboard there instead," he said, "that's a substitute."

He compared himself to the cardboard, apologized for the absence of the designated speaker, and then went on to give a long and scholarly talk. After the meeting, a good woman of the congregation, wanting to compliment him, rushed up, shook hands, and said, "You were no substitute—you were a real pane!"

* * *

Every talk has three basic elements: faith, hope, and charity. When the speaker begins the audience must have faith—faith that the talk will be interesting. After he has spoken for a few minutes, they display hope—hope that the end of it is drawing nigh. When the speaker is finally done, the congregation says "Amen." That is charity.

* * *

The speaker stood up in sacrament meeting. "Good afternoon," he said, speaking loudly. "Can you in the back hear me?" He continued with his talk. Every few minutes he repeated his question: "Can you hear me in the back?" Finally a deacon on the front row stood up. "I don't know about them, but I can hear fine if someone wants to trade places."

* * *

At a banquet, a speaker was ranting on about a subject which held very little interest for most of the audience. Unable to stand it any longer, one of them slipped quietly out. Just outside the door he bumped into another sufferer who had gone out just before him.

"Has he finished yet?" he was asked.

"Yes," said the man who had just escaped, "long ago, but he won't stop talking."

* * *

A bishop tells of the Sunday morning when he was approached after church by an old woman, who said in a tone of appreciation, "Bishop, you'll never know what your talk meant to me. It was just like water to a drowning man!"

* * *

A woman asked her husband, a high councilor who had been speaking at another ward, "How did your talk go?"

"Which one?" he asked. "The one I was going to give, the one I did give, or the one I delivered so brilliantly on the way home in the car?"

* * *

A bishop tended to talk too long in church, and the ward members were looking for a tactful way to tell him. One Sunday he came to church with a bandage on his finger, and someone asked him, "Bishop, how did you cut yourself?"

He replied, "I was thinking about my talk, and I cut my finger."

"Oh, I see," said the member. "Well, next time maybe you should think about your finger and cut your talk."

* * *

One Sunday in January, it was so cold and snowy that a Wyoming bishop found that only one person had arrived at church for sacrament meeting. "What do you think we should do, Brother Lewis, since we only have a congregation of one?"

"Well, Bishop," drawled the cattle rancher, "I don't know much about being a bishop. But one thing I know: when I promise my cattle a load of hay, I always keep my promise."

"You're right, of course," said the bishop. "Sit down in the first row here, and we'll have a meeting."

When it came time for the speakers on the program, the bishop, being the only ward leader present, took the place of all the sacrament meeting speakers. In fact, he got so long-winded that the meeting went on and on, far past the usual hour and ten minutes. After the closing prayer, the bishop said, "Well, Brother Lewis, what did you think of my talk?"

"Well, Bishop," said the rancher, "I don't know all that much about sacrament meeting talks—but one thing I know: when I promise my cattle a load of hay and only one shows up, I don't give it the whole load."

*   P O E M S   *

I hold that speaker great—
A truly fine narrator—
Who says, "It's getting late"
And doesn't make it later;
Whose talk is no infusion
Of long, trite platitudes,
Who says, "And in conclusion,"
And truly does *conclude.*

*   *   *

I love a finished speaker,
I mean I really do.
I don't mean one that's polished—
But one that's really through.

* Q U O T A T I O N S *

J. Golden Kimball: Now, what I am trying to get at is this: It takes intelligent people to understand what I am trying to get at. I do not do your thinking for you; you have to do your own thinking. If I give you a little chaff to get you to take a little wheat, my trouble has always been, you choose the chaff and leave the wheat (Conference Report, Apr. 1932, 78).

* * *

Mark Twain: What a good thing Adam had: When he said a good thing, he knew nobody had said it before.

* * *

Josh Billings: I don't care how much a man talks, if he only says it in a few words.

* * *

J. Golden Kimball: I am not accustomed to speaking to audiences out of doors. I have always had them closed in where they could not get away (Conference Report, Oct. 1918, 133).

* * *

J. Golden Kimball: If the brethren and sisters desire me to run smoothly and make no breaks, it will be advisable to keep awake until I finish my speech. . . . For me to be my natural self is somewhat dangerous, and to be original would cause the very air to resound with criticism. I fully realize that brevity, and to the point, should be added to the virtues. Horace Greeley used to say that the way to write a good editorial was to write it to the best of your ability, then cut it in two in the middle and print the last half. I am going to follow this suggestion (Conference Report, Apr. 1923, 125).

* * *

J. Golden Kimball: A little fellow was sick and he went to the doctor who was a herbalist. The doctor gave him four herbs and told him to boil them in a quart of water and drink it all. The little fellow said: "I can't. I only hold a pint." I am wondering how much you people hold? (Conference Report, Apr. 1929, 127).

* * *

J. Golden Kimball: I am ready to confess that I am keyed up to a pretty high tension, and the only thing I am afraid of is that I will say just what I think, which would be unwise, no doubt (Conference Report, Apr. 1904, 28).

* * *

Brigham Young: It is a great fault in the Elders of Israel, when they talk to a congregation, that they speak a great while about something, but you cannot always easily tell what. It may be more or less natural for some to do this, but it is a habit which can be overcome (*Journal of Discourses* 4:368).

* * *

Brigham Young: Brethren and sisters, I will make one request of you. When you speak, speak so that we can hear and understand you, whether it be much or little, good or bad. If you have nothing to say, take my counsel, and keep your seat. If you have anything to say, say it; and when you get through, stop (*Journal of Discourses* 7:270).

* * *

Brigham Young: I will take the liberty of suggesting to my brethren who address the congregation that our sermons should be short, and if they are not filled with life and spirit let them be shorter (*Journal of Discourses* 12:27).

* * *

George Eliot: Blessed is the man who, having nothing to say, abstains from giving us wordy evidence of the fact.

* * *

Rudger Clawson: There is a large clock in the other end of this building, that is greatly illuminated. It is placed there for the benefit and help of the speakers. When I am sitting on my seat I can see the time clearly, but when I arise to speak in this great building, in the midst of this great congregation, I regret to say I go blind and cannot see the time (Conference Report, Oct. 1922, 180).

* * *

Richard L. Evans: When I came to my present calling in the Church I thought perhaps I should make something of a reputation in some field or another, and I looked around to see what records might be available that could be acquired. I saw that some of my brethren had acquired, justifiably, a reputation for being authorities in the field of doctrine—some were trained in the professions—some in law, some in the sciences; and I concluded that about the only record that was left for me to strive for was that of brevity of expression, but I anticipated no such cooperation from the presiding offi-cer in helping me to achieve this record as I have had here today (Conference Report, Apr. 1940, 145).

* * *

Joseph F. Smith: As a boy I used to marvel when my father said that at the general conference he lost his appetite, and when he was called upon to speak, his arms, his elbows, and his hands went numb. I now look upon my father as a man of unusual fortitude. . . . I have felt that I was in danger of imminent disintegration south of my Adam's apple (Conference Report, Apr. 1943, 75).

* * *

George A. Smith: When I was about twenty-one years old I went on a mission, in company with Elder Don C. Smith, the youngest brother of the Prophet Joseph, through the States of Kentucky and Tennessee. When he rose to preach he wished to see a pretty good sized assembly, and to talk at least a couple of hours; when it was my turn to speak, some thirty minutes, perhaps, was as much time as I would wish to occupy. We occasionally had a small assembly, then Don would say, "Come, George A., you are good at preaching a picayune sermon; suppose you try this time."

It would seem to-day as though a picayune sermon would not answer the purpose, if the size of the congregation is the scale in which the discourse should be weighed (*Journal of Discourses* 3:280).

* * *

George A. Smith: I have offered these remarks, on the subject of policy, in rather a rambling manner, something like the parson, who was told that he did not speak to his text, "Very well," says he, "scattering shots hit the most birds" (*Journal of Discourses* 3:291).

* * *

Don B. Colton: A few Sundays ago in a conference a fine lady came up at the close of the meeting and expressed great appreciation of the services.

Some one asked her what part of the meeting she enjoyed best. She said, "Not the main speaker" (I was he) (Conference Report, Apr. 1936, 111).

* * *

Charles W. Nibley: My brethren and sisters, I suppose one could never grow old enough, at least I never expect to, to get entirely over stage fright. This is the third day that I have been sitting before this congregation, not knowing at what hour I might be called upon; and when one has gone through that experience for two or three days the stage fright becomes accentuated.

It is recorded of Thomas Carlyle, who could not do his thinking if there were any great noise about, that he had a neighbor, a lady, who kept some chickens; and the crowing of the roosters was a source of annoyance to him. He sent a kind letter to his neighbor and offered to buy the chickens so that he might kill them. She refused to let him have them, and said: "Besides I don't see why they bother you. The roosters crow only at stated intervals." He replied: "Yes, madam, that is true; but you don't know what I suffer waiting for them to crow" (Conference Report, Oct. 1924, 93).

* * *

Ezra T. Benson (after waiting for his turn to speak in general conference): I think I know now, brethren, how effectively suspense might be used as a tool of punishment (Conference Report, Apr. 1944, 54).

* * *

Marvin O. Ashton (upon being called upon to speak): I once heard of a man who put on his tombstone, "I expected this, but not so soon" (Conference Report, Oct. 1943, 21).

* * *

Heber J. Grant: I should very much like to occupy the other twenty minutes, but I firmly believe that if you hire a man to do a certain work, and he knows how to do it and you do not, it is a wise thing to let him do it. Now, I have a very dear friend who is my doctor, George W. Middleton, and he tells me that 40 or 45 minute speeches should be about my limit, and I have only two more minutes (Conference Report, Apr. 1937, 18).

* * *

Brigham Young: The kingdom of our God, that is set upon the earth, does not require men of many words and flaming oratorical talents, to establish truth and righteousness. It is not the many words that accomplish the designs of our Father in heaven, with Him it is the acts of the people more than their words; this I was convinced of, before I embraced the Gospel. Had it not been that I clearly saw and understood that the Lord Almighty would take the weak things of this world to confound the mighty, the wise, and the talented, there was nothing that could have induced me, or persuaded me to have ever become a public speaker (*Journal of Discourses* 4:20–21).

* * *

Marvin O. Ashton: A typical young Mormon boy in one of the wards the other night made a talk. I had a copy of that talk given me by a friend, because she thought that maybe I might be interested in it. The boy started out something like this:

"I am going to be frank, I want to be. I hope that I am understood." . . . He continued: "Generally when I am asked to give a talk in Church—a few days ahead Pa writes it, Ma corrects it and then Bill runs it off on the typewriter. Then, of course, I learn it off by heart. Now tonight I am not going to do that. I am going to speak just the way I feel." And by the way, I think we ought to encourage more of that kind of talks than we do; we ought to encourage originality; we ought to encourage people to have the courage of their convictions and say what they think. You know, if more talks were given extemporaneously we would get closer to the hearts of the people. Even Mark Twain said he believed in extemporaneous talks. He said he had been studying on one for fifteen years. When he got a chance, he said he wanted to give it. . . . Now, I believe that (Conference Report, Apr. 1943, 30–31).

* * *

Hugh B. Brown: For a speech to be immortal it does not need to be everlasting (Conference Report, Apr. 1956, 103).

* * *

Speaking of a lawyer, Abraham Lincoln said, "He can compress the most words into the smallest ideas better than any man I ever met."

* * *

Heber J. Grant: I am going to take as long as I want, you know, and if anybody gets tired and wants to go out he or she has my permission. Being an insurance agent I am not easily offended (Conference Report, Oct. 1941, 145).

* * *

Thomas E. McKay: While at luncheon today with my family, there was a lull in the conversation, and one of my daughters remarked that she hoped daddy would be called upon in this afternoon's session, so he could quit worrying and "join with us in conversation" (Conference Report, Oct. 1943, 60).

* * *

Marion G. Romney: A grandfather I once knew . . . was getting along in years and some people thought he didn't know when to quit talking. At a ward gathering they thought they shouldn't call on him because he would speak too long. Their final decision was, however, that they couldn't pass him by, so they called on him and asked him to stand and tell them in just a word how they could live to be as old as he was and still be of service. So he got up and said, "Keep breathing" (*Ensign*, Nov. 1982, 91).

* S T O R I E S *

U.S. President Woodrow Wilson was once asked how long he took to prepare a ten-minute speech.

"Two weeks."

"How long for an hour speech?"

"One week."

"How long for a two-hour speech?"

"I am ready now."

* * *

President Franklin Delano Roosevelt gave the following advice to his son regarding making speeches: "Be sincere; be brief; be seated."

* * *

Sir Josiah Stamp, in a speech at the Chicago Club, expressed a hope that he wasn't talking too long. "I wouldn't like to be in the position of the parson," he explained, "who in the midst of an interminable sermon, suddenly stopped to chide: 'You know I don't mind a bit having you look at your watches to see what time it is, but it really annoys me when you put them up to your ears to see if they are still running.'"

* * *

When Dr. Walter Williams spoke in a Chinese university, an interpreter translated into Chinese symbols on a blackboard. Dr. Williams noted that the interpreter stopped writing during most of the speech and at the conclusion he asked why. "We only write when the speaker says something," was the reply.

* * *

Chauncey Depew once played a trick upon Mark Twain on an occasion when they were both to speak at a banquet. Twain spoke first for some twenty minutes and was received with great enthusiasm. When Depew's turn came, immediately afterwards, he said, "Mr. Toastmaster, Ladies and Gentlemen, before this dinner, Mark Twain and I made an agreement to trade speeches. He has just delivered mine and I'm grateful for the reception you have accorded it. I regret that I have lost his speech and cannot remember a thing he had to say."

He sat down with much applause.

* * *

"I ought not to be surprised by anything at my time of life," said an aging bishop, "but one ward member did manage to take my breath away. I was giving a talk in Sacrament meeting about the Father's tender wisdom in caring for us all; illustrated by saying that the Father knows which of us grows best in sunlight and which of us must have shade. 'You know you plant roses in the sunshine,' I said, 'and heliotrope and geraniums; but if you want your fuchsias to grow they must be kept in a shady nook.' After my talk, which I hoped would be a comforting one, a woman came up to me, her face glowing with pleasure that was evidently deep and true. 'Oh, Bishop, I am so grateful for that talk,' she said, clasping my hand and shaking it warmly. My heart glowed for a moment, while I wondered what tender place in her heart and life I had touched. Only for a moment, though. 'Yes,' she went on fervently, 'I never knew before what was the matter with my fuchsias.'"

* * *

In J. Golden Kimball's day, the General Authorities were not told in advance when they would be called on to speak in general conference. In 1921, toward the end of three days of meetings, Brother Kimball's call finally came. He began, "My brethren and sisters, I have been hanging on the hook so long during this conference that I am nearly exhausted. I have had some wonderful thoughts, but have waited so long they have nearly all oozed out of me" (see Conference Report, Apr. 1921, 178).

* * *

General Alexander Smyth of Virginia was a man of much learning who filled his over-long speeches with far too many quotations. After giving one of his tiresome speeches in the Senate, he turned to Henry Clay, one of his colleagues, and said, "You, sir, speak for the present generation; but I speak for posterity."

"Yes," said Mr. Clay, "and you seem resolved to speak until the arrival of your audience."

* * *

The story is told of Wilton Lackaye who was scheduled to speak late on the program at a banquet at which all the speakers had been deathly long-winded.

The chairman introduced Lackaye, saying, "Wilton Lackaye, the famous actor, will now give you his address."

Lackaye faced the haggard audience and said, "Mr. Chairman, Ladies and Gentlemen, my address is the Lambs' Club, New York."

He sat down and received a tremendous ovation.

* * *

The well-known preacher, Charles Spurgeon, taught a class of religion students to be sure that their facial expressions harmonized with their message when they delivered sermons. "When you speak of heaven," he said, "let your face light up and be irradiated with a heavenly gleam. Let your eyes shine with reflected glory. And when you speak of hell—well, then your everyday face will do."

* * *

Governor Al Smith of New York agreed to speak to the inmates of Sing Sing prison. But when he stood on his feet he suddenly realized that he didn't know how to address them. "My fellow citizens," he said, then remembered that the prisoners had all lost their citizen-ship. Embarrassed he said, "My fellow convicts," but knew as soon as he said it that he had made another mistake. Finally he gave it up and said, "Well, in any case, I'm glad to see so many of you here."

* * *

A railroad maintenance man was notorious for his lengthy reports. Finally his supervisor wrote him an exasperated note: "For goodness sake, man, be brief!"

The reprimanded employee complied. His next report described the results of a flash flood: "Dear sir: Where the railroad was, the river is."

STATISTICS

* JOKES *

A hundred men and two women cooks worked at a logging camp. The foreman had been so wordy in his weekly reports that an execu-tive wrote to him, "We don't have time to read so many details. Boil it down. Just give us the percentages—that's what matters."

In his next report the foreman wrote, "Last month 1 per cent of the men married 50 per cent of the women."

* QUOTATIONS *

Richard L. Evans: I should like to close with one story, and I think maybe this is a good time to tell it. It is my favorite story on statistics.

I have told it in a number of places. It is not my story, but it belongs to Brother Roscoe Eardley. . . . Knowing of my interest in the subject, he stopped me one day and said, "I have the latest story on statistics for you. We were coming from California by automobile and we had all been over the road a number of times and were somewhat bored with it, and, as travelers often do to pass time, we began counting service stations. And we counted one for almost every mile along that almost eight hundred mile journey. But that is not the story. We were so busy counting service stations that we ran out of gas!"

I did not sympathize with him too much because he had already told me there was one service station for about every mile. Then he said, "That's statistics for you. Where we ran out it was about fifteen miles to the nearest gas pump!" (Conference Report, Apr. 1948, 169).

* STORIES *

You have probably heard the story of the father who had four daughters. As each of them left on a date one evening, he cautioned them to be home by midnight. The first returned at 11:45, the next at 11:50. The third came home at midnight, whereupon he locked the doors, turned out the lights, and went to bed. His wife reminded him that Mary had not come in yet. He said with great satisfaction, "Seventy-five percent of them are home—isn't that a pretty good percentage?" (Victor L. Brown, "Priesthood Activation," *Ensign*, May 1982, 34).

STRESS

* J O K E S *

Have you heard about the new tranquilizer? It doesn't help you relax, but it lets you enjoy being tense.

* S T O R I E S *

Dr. Truman Madsen, a member of the faculty of Brigham Young University . . . , once asked [Elder Richard L. Evans of the Quorum of the Twelve]: "How do you account for your composure, your serenity of soul, under the frenetic schedule you must keep?" Elder Evans' answer came back without hesitation: "Exhaustion!" (Evans, *Richard L. Evans,* 14).

SUCCESS

* P O E M S *

He that will thrive must rise at five;
He that hath thriven may lie till seven.

* S T O R I E S *

Asked one day for a mathematical formula for success in life, Albert Einstein gave the following:

"If *a* is success in life, the formula is, *a* equals *x* plus *y* plus *z*, *x* being work and *y* being play."

"And what is *z*?" he was asked.

"*Z*," he said, "is keeping your mouth shut."

SUSTAINING

* Q U O T A T I O N S *

Brigham Young: The first name I shall present to you is that of Brigham Young, President of the Church of Jesus Christ of Latter-day Saints. If any person can say that he should not be sustained in this office, say so. If there is no objection, as it is usual in the marriage ceremony of the Church of England, "Let them for ever afterwards hold their peace," and not go snivelling around, saying that you would like to have a better man (*Journal of Discourses* 7:228).

* * *

In the October 1954 General Conference, President J. Reuben Clark, during the sustaining of officers, presented the name of David O. McKay as prophet, seer and revelator, and president of The Church of Jesus Christ of Latter-day Saints. All present voted in the affirmative. President Clark overlooked asking for a negative vote, and upon being reminded by President McKay that he should do so, he made the following comment: "Excuse me, I did not see anything but all upraised hands. If anybody wants to vote negative, now is your opportunity." President George Albert Smith, on a similar occasion, said, "All who want to vote negatively, raise the left hand" (Conference Report, Oct. 1954, 115).

* * *

J. Golden Kimball: I sustain and uphold with all my heart and soul President Heber J. Grant as prophet of God. It was only two months ago that a young lawyer—I suppose he considers himself one of the brilliant young lawyers—undertook to criticize severely the President of the Church. I was somewhat disturbed. I said, "I am going to take out my watch and give you five minutes to name a better man." I haven't heard from him yet (Conference Report, Apr. 1930, 61).

* * *

Marion G. Romney: It is an easy thing to believe in the dead prophets, but it is a greater thing to believe in the living prophets. I will give you an illustration.

One day when President [Heber J.] Grant was living, I sat in my office across the street following a general conference. A man came over to see me, an elderly man. He was very upset about what had been said in this conference by some of the Brethren, including myself. I could tell from his speech that he came from a foreign land. After I had quieted him enough so he would listen, I said, "Why did you come to America?" "I am here because a prophet of God told me to come." "Who was the prophet;" I continued. "Wilford Woodruff." "Do you believe Wilford Woodruff was a prophet of God?" "Yes, I do." "Do you believe that President Joseph F. Smith was a prophet of God?" "Yes, sir."

Then came the sixty-four dollar question. "Do you believe that Heber J. Grant is a prophet of God?" His answer, "I think he ought to keep his mouth shut about old age assistance" (Conference Report, Apr. 1953, 125).

* * *

J. Golden Kimball: I was conversing with a prominent stranger yesterday, and he told me he was prejudiced when he came here, and I said: "I wish you had known our leading men. I wish you had been acquainted with Brigham Young and Heber C. Kimball; you would have liked them."

He said, "Do you think so?"

I replied, "I know you would, or else you are not a man like I am" (Conference Report, Oct. 1912, 29).

* * *

Ben E. Rich: May God bless this work; may God bless the prophets, seers, and revelators who rule over it. May we always love them, and let the world know that we do love them, and not be ashamed of it. I would rather take the counsel and advice of President Joseph F. Smith than that of any man on this earth; and if some people don't like it, they can lump it (Conference Report, Apr. 1910, 92).

SWEARING

* QUOTATIONS *

Heber J. Grant: I have heard it said that "damn" is not swearing, that it is only emphasis. I was preaching one night with the late President John Henry Smith, in the opera house in Phoenix. The legislature was in session. Hearing that two of the "Mormon" apostles were there, some of the members of the legislature waited on us and said they had arranged to hire the opera house, and they would agree to fill it if we would condescend to preach. Well, we usually hire our own hall and condescend to preach to empty benches; so, of course, we condescended, and were delighted with the opportunity. One of the good sisters who came down from Mesa was sitting behind a man while I was preaching, and she heard him say, with emphasis, that I was an earnest preacher. Pretty soon, with that emphasis again, he said I was a good preacher, and finally once more with emphasis he said: "That man believes (with emphasis) every word he is saying." I ask no greater compliment (Conference Report, Oct. 1922, 13).

* * *

George A. Smith: There is an idea out that a man who has to go to the canyon cannot do it without swearing, or that when he gets to the mouth of the canyon he must throw off his religion and swear all the way up and back again. Any man who entertains such a sentiment should dispense with it at once, for he needs his religion more there than anywhere else. The roads are rough, and there is danger of him being tipped over and breaking his neck, or mashing up his wagon or his team, and he needs the influence of his religion as much under such circumstances as under any others. The Elders of Israel should avoid indulging in rough language under all circumstances. Most men, if they thought there was a probability of them dying by some sudden accident, would begin to think about praying. When a man is more exposed to danger than at any other time I am sure he needs his religion, for if he should have a log roll over him, and be sent into eternity with a big oath in his mouth, he might not be recognized as a Saint on the other side of the veil (*Journal of Discourses* 12:138–40).

* * *

Daniel Hess: On some rare occasions, . . . we may be moved by the Spirit to let someone know his language is unacceptable.

I faced such a moment while in the [U.S.] navy. We were in boot camp with a company of men who constantly bragged in the foulest language about the evil things they had done. One day a friend and I were sitting on our bunks when the door suddenly burst open and in came one of the roughest sailors. He started to call our Savior dirty, derogatory names. My friend looked at me and said, "Dan, we're not going to take that, are we?" I thought about it for a minute, and finally said, "I guess not." So I stepped out in front of the man as he came down through the rows of beds, and I told him that I loved the Savior and that he couldn't say those things about him. Now it was his turn to think it over for a minute, but in the end he apologized. I'd like to think, for his sake, that it wasn't just because I happened to be the camp boxing champion (*Time of Your Life*, 109–10).

* STORIES *

Just before playing golf in Georgia, President Dwight D. Eisenhower remarked, "You're going to hear a lot of laughing today. My doctor has given me orders that if I don't start laughing instead of cussing when I miss those shots, then he's going to stop me from playing golf. So every time I miss a shot today, I'm going to go ho-ho-ho."

* * *

A young dairyman in Idaho, inactive in the Church, was complaining about J. Golden Kimball's swearing.

"Don't you swear?" asked a friend, knowing well he did.

"Yes, I do," answered the friend, "but I ain't goin' to heaven" (Cheney, *Golden Legacy*, 31).

* * *

One woman, hoping to help J. Golden Kimball break his habit of swearing, held up President Heber J. Grant as an example. "Brother Kimball," she said, "have you ever heard President Grant swear?"

"Just once," Brother Kimball replied. "He and I were in St. George together during the depression. It was summer, the crops were dying for want of water, the people were starving. We prayed with them for rain, but our prayers were not answered. I said, 'It's a ——ed shame!' and President Grant said, 'Yes, it is'" (Cheney, *Golden Legacy*, 121).

TEACHING

* JOKES *

First Primary teacher: Is the Jones boy hard to handle in class?
Second Primary teacher: I'll say! Not only is he the naughtiest kid in class—he's also the one with the perfect attendance record!

TEASING

* STORIES *

Spencer W. Kimball loved to tease. For example, he would say to one of his children, "I see you are in the newspaper!"

"Where? Where?"

"It says right here, 'Crowd of Thousands Watches Parade'" (Kimball, "Spencer W. Kimball," *BYU Studies* 25[4]: 62).

TECHNOLOGY

* STORIES *

Once when Spencer W. Kimball was too weak to shave, a nurse shaved him with an electric shaver, but with no apparent effect. Finally he suggested, "Perhaps it would work better if you took the cap off" (Kimball, "Spencer W. Kimball," *BYU Studies* 25[4]: 66).

TEMPTATION

* QUOTATIONS *

Moses Thatcher: I heard a story in regard to a brother in Farmington, a few years ago. The question of gathering the poor Saints from England came up in an evening meeting. The brother had two cows, and he donated one for the purpose mentioned. In going home a spirit of darkness said unto him: "You have been very foolish. You have given away one of the two cows you possessed, while Brother so-and-so, a much wealthier man than you, has only given five dollars. Now, you have done a wrong thing, a foolish thing." And thus was this brother tempted until he turned round and said, as though addressing himself to Satan: "If you don't cease tempting me, I will go back to the Bishop, and give him the other one" (*Journal of Discourses* 24:302).

* * *

Brigham Young: The Gospel of salvation has been revealed unto us expressly to teach our hearts understanding, and when I learn the principles of charity or righteousness I will adhere to them, and say to selfishness, you must not have that which you want, and when it urges that I have no more flour than I shall need until harvest, and that I must not give any away, not even a pound, I say, get out of my door. And when it argues that a brother will not be profited by our endeavors to benefit him, that you had better keep your money to yourselves and not let him have this ox, that farm or cow, &c., and strives to persuade you not to feed such a poor person, not to do anything for the P. E. F. Company, that you have not any more than you need, just do as the man did in Vermont, for by the report we would judge him to be a pretty good man. He had a farm, raised a large quantity of grain, and usually had some to spare. It so happened one season that a poor neighbor thrashed out his rye, and was to receive his pay in grain. The poor man came; the farmer told him to leave his bags and he would measure up the amount and have it ready when again called for. He was alone when measuring the grain, and as he put into the measure, something whispered to him, "Pour it in lightly," but instead of doing this, he gave the measure a kick. When he put on the strike something said to him, "When you take that off, take a little out; the poor man will know nothing about it." At last the farmer said, "Mr. Devil, walk out of my barn, or I will heap every half bushel I measure for the poor man."

When you are tempted to do wrong, do not stop one moment to argue, but tell Mr. Devil to walk out of your barn, or you will heap up every half bushel; you can do that I know (*Journal of Discourses* 3:358–59).

Testimony

* J O K E S *

He said he didn't lose his testimony; instead, he got so open-minded it just fell out.

* Q U O T A T I O N S *

Testimony at a youth conference: Oh, this gospel is so true I just can't believe it!

* S T O R I E S *

Called to be president of the Tooele, Utah, Stake at the age of twenty-four, [Heber J. Grant] delivered a short speech because [he] "ran out of ideas."

Joseph F. Smith commented, "Heber, you said you believe the gospel with all your heart, and propose to live it, but you did not bear your testimony that you know it is true. Don't you know absolutely that this gospel is true?"

"I do not."

"What, you! A president of a stake?"

"That is what I said."

"President [John] Taylor," said Joseph F., "I am in favor of undoing this afternoon what we did this morning. I do not think any man should preside over a stake who has not a perfect and abiding knowledge of the divinity of this work."

To this Heber replied, "I am not going to complain."

"President Taylor," Heber J. Grant recalled, "had a habit, when something pleased him excessively, of shaking his body and laughing," and he said to President Smith, "Joseph, Joseph, Joseph, he knows it just as well as you do. The only thing that he does not know is that he does know it. . . . You do not need to worry" (see Van Wagoner and Walker, *A Book of Mormons,* 100).

TIME

* STORIES *

Joseph Fielding Smith was so conscious of time and so determined to use it wisely that he "wore two watches, one on each wrist, and kept another pair in reserve. He was up every morning before six and worked hard all day long. One of his sons recalls, 'Somehow it seemed immoral to lie in bed after 6. Of course, I only tried it once. Father saw to that.' One of President Smith's maxims was 'People die in bed. And so does ambition'" (West, *Profiles of the Presidents,* 251–52).

TITHES AND OFFERINGS

* JOKES *

On Sunday morning a father gave his son two quarters and a dollar. "Give the bishop the dollar for our fast offerings," the father said. "You can keep the quarters for your allowance."

When the dad saw the boy in sacrament meeting he still had the dollar. "Why didn't you give the dollar to the bishop like I asked?" the father asked.

"Well, in Primary Sister Goode said that God loves a cheerful giver. So I gave the bishop the fifty cents. I knew I could be a lot more cheerful about that than giving him the whole dollar."

* * *

Bishop's encouragement for members to increase fast offerings: I would like to remind you that what the Lord asks you to give is deductible; it cannot be taken with you; and the love of it is the root of all evil.

* * *

As a young man, Brother Jones made $100 a week and faithfully paid $10 tithing. As he grew older, his business prospered. When he earned $500 a week, he paid $50 tithing. When he earned $1,000 a week, he paid $100 tithing. Soon, his tithing amounted to $500 a week. When his bishop visited his palatial home, Brother Jones complained, "I just don't feel good about paying $500 tithing a week. That's a lot of money." The bishop replied, "I can understand that, but why don't we pray about it?" "What good would that do?" "Well, we could ask the Lord to reduce your income to the point where you felt good about paying tithing again."

* QUOTATIONS *

Alexander Toponce: In [pioneer] days if you wanted to go to the theatre you took butter, eggs, chickens, potatoes, wheat, anything like that to a tithing house, and they would give you script for it. Then you took the script to the theatre or to any store and bought what you wanted with it. On one occasion, I took a big fat turkey up to the tithing yard to sell for script and the tithing clerk had gone to supper.

I waited and he did not return, so I had to go and get the young lady I had invited to go with me, and I carried the turkey into the window of the box office and asked for two balcony seats. That clerk at the window handed out the two tickets and two spring chickens for change and I had to sit there all through the performance with a chicken under each arm and the young lady I was with was quite peeved that I paid so little attention to her. I was never so embarrassed and uncomfortable in all my life (*Reminiscences of Alexander Toponce,* 186–87).

* * *

Charles W. Nibley: I think it is Brother Golden Kimball who tells the story of his father's owning a beautiful horse. Tithing was paid with horses, cattle, sheep, and everything obtainable in those days. The horse Brother Kimball had was a very fine one, and he said to the boys: "I believe I will turn that horse in for tithing; pay it to Bishop Hunter." The next morning one of the boys paraded the beautiful animal around and wanted to keep it, but President Kimball said: "See here, you take that horse right down and pay it in for tithing, before my heart puckers up" (Conference Report, Oct. 1924, 97).

* * *

Brigham Young: Talk about this people being poor, why we will get so rich by and by that we will refuse to pay our taxes; we have got so rich now that we cannot pay our tithing (*Journal of Discourses* 15:20–21).

TRUST

* QUOTATIONS *

Heber J. Grant: I endorse what Brother Merrill has said here today, and what our last speaker, Brother Bowen, has said. I noticed that Brother Bowen laid down several sheets of paper and did not read what was on them. I hope that when he turns in his manuscript for publication he will put it all in, because I endorse everything that he said and I endorse what he was going to say, without knowing what it was (Conference Report, Oct. 1941, 143).

TRUTH

* QUOTATIONS *

Orson Hyde: Brother Taylor said, the other day, that it was right to gather truth from every source. If the Devil has got truth, then it is right to secure it. [President Brigham Young: "What truth he has he has stolen."] We have a right to gather up truth just on the same principle that the United States gather up property that is marked U.S. You know when they go through the land and find anything with U.S. on it, they take it. So likewise, when we find any truth with U, S, US on, we claim it as our own. It belongs to US (*Journal of Discourses* 8:25).

* * *

Brigham Young: Brother [Orson] Hyde . . . once, . . . in conversation with brother Joseph Smith advanced the idea that eternity or boundless space was filled with the Spirit of God, or the Holy Ghost. After portraying his views upon that theory very carefully and minutely, he asked brother Joseph what he thought of it? He replied that it appeared very beautiful, and that he did not know of but one serious objection to it. Says brother Hyde, "What is that?" Joseph replied, "it is not true" (*Journal of Discourses* 4:266).

* STORIES *

On one occasion, having failed to make a stubborn opponent see the error of his reasoning, Abraham Lincoln said, "Well, let's see. How many legs does a cow have?"

"Four, of course," his opponent replied.

"That's right," answered Lincoln. "Now suppose we call the cow's tail a leg, how many legs would the cow have then?"

"Why, five, of course."

"That's where you make an error," said Lincoln. "Simply calling the cow's tail a leg doesn't make it a leg."

WEATHER

* QUOTATIONS *

Rudger Clawson: Brethren and sisters, the Lord is very good to us and orders all things well. Last evening He sent a beautiful shower which cooled the air and laid the dust, and today it is bright and beautiful for the holding of our conference. . . . Speaking of the weather reminds me of a story that is told of a capitalist who went from the eastern states into one of the western states—Kansas, I think—to look at a large farm, with a view to investment. In speaking with the farmer, he inquired very carefully as to the quality of the soil of the farm; the farmer replied that it was very rich and productive. The capitalist said, "How is the weather here, how is your climate?" "O," he says, "we have a very fine climate here—very fine. I will give you an example: Sometime ago I had two or three hundred chickens that I wanted to put upon the market. Being very busy, I did not know what to do to prepare these chickens and get them to the market. I was very much worried in regard to the matter. About that time a cyclone came along, caught up the chickens, twisted their necks, stripped them of all their feathers, and transported them to the town, ten miles distant, and put them on the market, all ready for sale the next morning" (Conference Report, Oct. 1909, 64).

WELFARE

* QUOTATIONS *

Heber J. Grant: I read of one good lady up in Dakota who said, if one of her hogs was sick, or if anything was the matter with any of the fruits, or flowers, or vegetables and garden truck, if there were troublesome insects or anything of that nature, all she had to do was to send down to Washington, and the Agricultural Department would supply her with information how to cure the hog or protect the plants in her garden. But, if her husband, her son or her daughter was sick, and she should write to the Government, she could not get any information or help. Moral: Be a hog, and the Government will take care of you, if you get sick (Conference Report, Apr. 1911, 24).

WISDOM

* QUOTATIONS *

J. Golden Kimball: It is considered a good thing to look wise, especially when not over burdened with information (Conference Report, Apr. 1906, 74).

WORD OF WISDOM

* JOKES *

One day in Gospel Doctrine class, the over-enthusiastic teacher began preaching the gospel of natural foods. He gave it as his opinion that the preservatives in store-bought foods were against the Word of Wisdom.

One of the older ward members raised her hand and commented, "At my age I'd better steer clear of those natural foods, then. I need all the preservatives I can get!"

* * *

The missionaries, tracting out a small country town, stopped to chat with a little old man in a rocking chair on his front porch. "You look pretty good," one missionary said. "How have you managed to live so long?"

"Well," the man wheezed, "every day I smoke my pipe, I down a quart of moonshine, and I drink lots of coffee."

"That's terrible! How old are you anyway?"

"Thirty."

* * *

After a sermon on the Word of Wisdom, a man approached the speaker. "That was the first talk on the Word of Wisdom I ever enjoyed," he said.

"Why is that?" the speaker asked.

"Because now I'm keeping the Word of Wisdom."

* QUOTATIONS *

Brigham Young: It is a loathsome practice to use tobacco in any way. A doctor told an old lady in New York, when she insisted upon his telling her whether snuff would injure her brain, "It will not hurt the brain: there is no fear of snuff's hurting the brain of anyone, for no person that has brains will take snuff" (*Journal of Discourses* 9:35–36).

* * *

Joseph F. Smith: One thing I deplore, and that is the fact that I can scarcely go onto the street or side-walk but I see one to a dozen or more boys in their 'teens—with pipes of tobacco in their mouths, puffing away in the open. When I see them, I think, Oh! what a pity, oh! what a shame! How foolish, how imbecile, how useless, and how injurious is this practice to the youth of the people. I deplore the sight of it wherever I see it; I want to tell those present, who are in the habit of using these things, that when you meet me in the street with a pipe, cigarette, or a cigar in your mouths, please do not recognize me—go right by, and I will do the same. I never did like to bow to a nasty, old, stinking pipe, nor to take my hat off to it (Conference Report, Apr. 1910, 7).

* * *

Heber J. Grant: According to the Kansas City Star, Mrs. James Watson, editor and publisher of the Dearborn, Mo., Democrat, has the following suggestion to make to booze fighters: "To the married man who cannot get along without his drinks, we suggest the following as a means to freedom from the bondage of the habit: Start a saloon in your own house. Be the only customer. You will have no license to pay. Go to your wife and give her $2 to buy a gallon of whiskey, and remember there are sixty-nine drinks in one gallon. Buy your drinks from no one except your wife, and by the time the first gallon is gone she will have $8 to put in the bank and $2 to start business again. Should you live ten years and continue to buy booze from her and then die with snakes in your boots, she will have money to bury you decently, educate your children, buy a house and lot and marry a decent man and quit thinking about you" (Conference Report, Apr. 1916, 97).

*   S T O R I E S   *

Once a flight attendant asked Spencer W. Kimball, "Would you like something to drink?"

"What do you have?" he asked.

"Coffee, tea, Coca-Cola."

He shook his head. "Do you have any lemonade?"

"No," she said, "but I could squeeze you a little."

He recoiled in mock dismay: "Don't you squeeze me!" (Kimball, "Spencer W. Kimball," *BYU Studies* 25[4]: 68).

WORK

* JOKES *

God put me on earth to accomplish a certain number of things.
Right now I am so far behind, I will never die!

* * *

A poor but learned man was working on a Bible commentary. His
pragmatic friend said, "How impractical! Why don't you stop writing?
It will get you nowhere!"

"And if I stopped writing—would it get me anywhere?" asked the
scholar.

* QUOTATIONS *

J. Golden Kimball: Do you want eternal life? Almost everybody
here would be awfully keen for it, if it did not cost anything. We would
accept the whole world if it did not cost anything; I would be willing
to take half of it myself (Conference Report, Apr. 1915, 79).

* STORIES *

When Spencer W. Kimball visited Italy, he asked why no one had
arranged for him to meet with the missionaries. He was told they were
trying not to overtax him. He said, "I know what you are trying to do,
you are trying to save me. But I don't want to be saved, I want to be
exalted" (Kimball, "Spencer W. Kimball," *BYU Studies* 25[4]: 70).

* * *

Once when Paderewski played before Queen Victoria, the sovereign exclaimed with enthusiasm, "Mr. Paderewski, you are a genius!"

"Ah, Your Majesty," he replied, "that may be, but before I was a genius, I was a drudge."

* * *

A woman from Ogden traveled for the first time over the mountains from Logan, Utah, to Bear Lake. She was struck with the lake's beautiful turquoise color. Later, in general conference, she heard J. Golden Kimball say he had pioneered on a ranch near Bear Lake. Buttonholing him after conference, she asked, "Wasn't it wonderful to go over the mountain and see that exquisite lake?"

Brother Kimball answered, "If I had known it was going to be famous for its beauty, I'd have looked at it" (Cheney, *Golden Legacy*, 109).

* * *

Spencer W. Kimball was always humble about his position. After serving for five years as president of the Church, he said, "I still wonder what was the Lord thinking about, making a little country boy like me [president of his church], unless he knew that I didn't have any sense and would just keep on working" (Kimball, "Spencer W. Kimball," *BYU Studies* 25[4]: 62).

* * *

The great inventor Thomas Edison showed his love of work when his wife complained that he was working too hard and needed a rest. "You must go on a vacation," she declared.

"But where would I go?" asked the inventor.

"Just decide where you'd rather be than anywhere else on earth, and then go there," Mrs. Edison suggested.

"Very well," Edison said. "I will go there tomorrow."

The next morning Mrs. Edison found him back at work in his laboratory (see Reading, *Joy*, 177).

* * *

President Heber J. Grant, concerned that Elder James E. Talmage was working too hard, constantly urged him to take up golf. Finally, Elder Talmage agreed to play until he hit a shot that President Grant rated as a "real golf shot." After that, he could decide for himself whether to continue.

The two went to a golf course, where President Grant gave a brief lesson on addressing the ball. Elder Talmage stepped up and hit it, and the ball sailed more than two hundred yards straight down the fairway. After President Grant had congratulated him on hitting "a real nice golf shot," Elder Talmage said, "If I have carried out my part of the agreement, then I shall call on you to live up to yours. I should like to get back to the office, where I have a great deal of work waiting." Then he put down the golf clubs and walked away (Van Wagoner and Walker, *A Book of Mormons*, 347).

* * *

[When Elder Spencer W. Kimball traveled] on weekend assignments to stake conferences he would stay in the home of the stake president or one of his counselors. . . .

At Rigby, Idaho, President Christensen put him up on Saturday night. When they got home about 10:00 P.M. from the chapel, Spencer asked his host for a jumper, overalls, old shoes and a hat. "Under a little pressure he agreed," said Spencer.

"I milked two of the three cows while he milked the other and did some feeding and then we went in and went to bed. Next morning I was up and dressed again in my old clothes with the milk bucket on my arm. In conference when he introduced me he told about my help. After the meeting people came up to shake hands and said,

'When you come next time you can stay with us'" (Kimball and Kimball, *Spencer W. Kimball,* 232).

WORRY

* JOKES *

Woman to psychiatrist: I'm concerned about my husband. He thinks he's a refrigerator.

Psychiatrist: Well, that's a rather harmless delusion. I wouldn't worry.

Woman: Maybe so. But he sleeps with his mouth open, and I can't get to sleep with that light on!

* * *

When I take a trip by plane, I think about three things—faith, hope and gravity.

* * *

Home teacher: Perhaps you're worrying too much, Sister Barnes.

Sister Barnes: I don't know why you'd say that. It must be helping me; ninety percent of the things I worry about never happen!

YOUTH

* JOKES *

Jason had just received his driver's license. "Dad," he said, "I'd like to be able to use the car."

"Well, son," his dad said, "I'll make a deal with you. Bring your grades up, study your scriptures better, and get your hair cut. Then we'll talk about it."

Three weeks later Jason pulled his dad aside. "Dad, can we talk about me using the car?"

"Son, I've been real proud of you," the father said. "You've brought your grades up and you've studied your scriptures diligently. But you didn't get your hair cut!"

Jason was ready with an answer. "Well, Dad, I've been thinking about that. Samson had long hair; Moses had long hair; even the first Twelve Apostles had long hair . . ."

"That's fine, Son," the father replied. "Of course, they walked everywhere they went."

* * *

A young woman went to visit her grandmother. The old lady was distressed by what she considered the girl's wild and unruly manners and speech. Not wishing to appear stern and demanding, she decided nevertheless that she should reprimand her granddaughter.

One evening as they were sitting together the old lady said gently, "Dear, there are just two words I want you to refrain from using. One is 'swell' and the other is 'lousy.'"

"All right," replied the girl agreeably, "What are they?"

* * *

A college-age daughter wrote home, "Dear Dad and Mom. I'm really worried about you. Haven't heard from you in weeks. Could you please put a check in the mail so I'll know you're all right?"

* * *

A family's college-age daughter called from BYU: "Mom, I need a hundred dollars. I've met this wonderful returned missionary. I've spent five Sundays in a row with him, and each time I wore one of the dresses I brought to college with me. Now it's coming up on the sixth Sunday, and I don't have any more dresses! Could you please send money for another dress?"

"I've got a better idea," her mom answered. "Get a new boyfriend, and you can start all over."

ZION

* QUOTATIONS *

Brigham Young: Where is the land of Zion? It is wherever the finger of the Lord has pointed out for His people to gather to. That is the place to go to. I recollect a lady asked me in Canada, in 1832 or '3, how large Jackson County was; and when I said 30 miles square, said she, "Suppose the whole world would embrace your doctrine, how would they get into Jackson County?" My reply was that, "Jackson County, in that case, would cover the whole world. Zion will expand as far as the necessity of the case requires it. You need not fear but there will be room for you, if you believe and gather with the Saints" (*Journal of Discourses* 12:28–29).

BIBLIOGRAPHY

A Time to Laugh: A Briggs Family Collection. Salt Lake City: Family Library Guild, 1987.

Ayre, J. Randolph. *Illustrations to Inspire*. Salt Lake City: Bookcraft, 1968.

Bitton, Davis. *Wit and Whimsy in Mormon History*. Salt Lake City: Deseret Book Co., 1974.

Manuscript History of Brigham Young, 1801–44. Elden J. Watson, ed. Salt Lake City: Smith Secretarial Service, 1968.

Brown, Hugh B. *An Abundant Life: The Memoirs of Hugh B. Brown*. Edwin B. Firmage, ed. Salt Lake City: Signature Books, 1988.

———. "Father, Are You There?" Audio Tape, 1959, Harold B. Lee Library, Brigham Young University, Provo, Utah.

Cheney, Thomas E. *The Golden Legacy*. Santa Barbara: Peregrine Smith, 1979.

Conference Reports of The Church of Jesus Christ of Latter-day Saints. Salt Lake City: The Church of Jesus Christ of Latter-day Saints.

Cowley, Matthew. *Matthew Cowley Speaks*. Salt Lake City: Deseret Book Co., 1954.

Durham, G. Homer. *N. Eldon Tanner: His Life and Service*. Salt Lake City: Deseret Book Co., 1982.

Durrant, George D. *Look at the Sky*. Salt Lake City: Bookcraft, 1994.

Evans, Richard L., Jr. *Richard L. Evans, the Man and the Message*. Salt Lake City: Bookcraft, 1973.

Eyre, Richard. *Don't Just Do Something: New Maxims to Refresh and Enrich Your Life*. New York: Simon and Schuster, 1995.

Edmunds, Mary Ellen. *Love Is a Verb*. Salt Lake City: Deseret Book Co., 1995.

Featherstone, Vaughn J. *Commitment*. Salt Lake City: Bookcraft, 1982.

Fife, Austin, and Alta Fife. *Saints of Sage and Saddle*. Bloomington: Indiana University, 1956.

Gibbons, Francis M. *David O. McKay: Apostle to the World, Prophet of God*. Salt Lake City: Deseret Book Co., 1986.

Grant, Heber J. *Gospel Standards.* G. Homer Durham, comp. Salt Lake City: Improvement Era, 1969.

Hartshorn, Leon R. *Classic Stories from the Lives of Our Prophets.* Salt Lake City: Deseret Book Co., 1988.

Hawkes, Sharlene Wells. *Living In but Not Of the World.* Salt Lake City: Deseret Book Co., 1997.

Hess, Daniel. "Tastes and Standards." *The Time of Your Life.* Salt Lake City: Bookcraft, 1977.

Howard, F. Burton. *Marion G. Romney, His Life and Faith.* Salt Lake City: Bookcraft, 1988.

Jack, Elaine L. *Eye to Eye, Heart to Heart.* Salt Lake City: Deseret Book Co., 1992.

Journal of Discourses. 26 vols. London: Latter-day Saints' Book Depot, 1853–1886.

Joy. Salt Lake City: Deseret Book Co., 1980.

Kapp, Ardeth Greene. *My Neighbor, My Sister, My Friend.* Salt Lake City: Deseret Book Co., 1990.

Kimball, Edward L. "Spencer W. Kimball, a Man of Good Humor," *BYU Studies* 25[4]: 59–70.

Kimball, Edward L., and Andrew E. Kimball, Jr. *Spencer W. Kimball.* Salt Lake City: Bookcraft, 1977.

Smith, Joseph Fielding. *Life of Joseph F. Smith.* Salt Lake City: Deseret Book Co., 1969.

Madsen, Carol Cornwall, and Susan Staker Oman. *Sisters and Little Saints.* Salt Lake City: Deseret Book Co., 1979.

Maxwell, Neal A. *Meek and Lowly.* Salt Lake City: Deseret Book Co., 1987.

McConkie, Joseph F. *True and Faithful: The Life Story of Joseph Fielding Smith.* Salt Lake City: Bookcraft 1971.

McKay, Llewelyn R. *Home Memories of President David O. McKay.* Salt Lake City: Deseret Book Co., 1956.

Morrell, Jeanette McKay. *Highlights in the Life of President David O. McKay.* Salt Lake City: Deseret Book Co., 1966.

Nash, Richard. *Lengthen Your Smile.* Salt Lake City: Deseret Book Co., 1996.

Packer, Boyd K. *Teach Ye Diligently.* Salt Lake City: Deseret Book Co., 1975.

Parry, Jay A., and Larry E. Morris. *Mormon Book of Lists.* Salt Lake City: Bookcraft, 1987.

Pratt, Parley P. *Autobiography of Parley P. Pratt.* Parley P. Pratt, Jr., ed. Salt Lake City: Deseret Book Co., 1985.

Sessions, Gene Allred. *Latter-day Patriots: Nine Mormon Families and Their Revolutionary War Heritage.* Salt Lake City: Deseret Book Co., 1975.

Smith, Joseph Fielding. *Take Heed to Yourselves!* Salt Lake City: Deseret Book Co., 1966.

Smith, Joseph Fielding, Jr., and John J. Stewart. *Life of Joseph Fielding Smith, Tenth President of The Church of Jesus Christ of Latter-day Saints.* Salt Lake City: Deseret Book Co., 1972.

Swinton, Heidi S. *In the Company of Prophets.* Salt Lake City: Deseret Book Co., 1993.

Tate, Lucile C. *LeGrand Richards, Beloved Apostle.* Salt Lake City: Bookcraft, 1982.

Taylor, John. *The Gospel Kingdom: Selections from the Writings and Discourses of John Taylor.* G. Homer Durham, comp. Salt Lake City: Bookcraft, 1943.

Taylor, Samuel W. *The Kingdom or Nothing: The Life of John Taylor, Militant Mormon.* New York: Macmillan, 1976.

Toponce, Alexander. *Reminiscences of Alexander Toponce.* Ogden, Utah: Mrs. Katie Toponce, 1923.

Van Wagoner, Richard S., and Steven C. Walker. *A Book of Mormons.* Salt Lake City: Signature Books, 1982.

West, Emerson Roy. *Profiles of the Presidents.* Salt Lake City: Deseret Book Co., 1980.

Whitney, Orson F. *Life of Heber C. Kimball.* Salt Lake City: Juvenile Instructor's Office, 1888.

INDEX